Dear Barbara,

May this book serve to develop your "Third Eye" & provide inspiration when evaluating all these picture books!

Best Wishes & Love,

Jan Lieberman
7/20/79

The Illustrated Book: *Its Art and Craft*

Books by Diana Klemin

THE ILLUSTRATED BOOK: ITS ART AND CRAFT
THE ART OF ART FOR CHILDREN'S BOOKS

The Illustrated Book: *Its Art and Craft*

by Diana Klemin

Bramhall House • New York

A DIVISION OF CLARKSON N. POTTER, INC.

Verse and illustration: From *Bestiary/Bestiario*, a poem by Pablo Neruda, translated by Elsa Neuberger
with woodcuts by Antonio Frasconi, English translation copyright © 1965 by HARCOURT, BRACE & WORLD, INC.,
illustrations copyright © 1965 by Antonio Frasconi, © 1958 by Editorial Losada, S.A., Buenos Aires.
Reproduced by permission of HARCOURT, BRACE & WORLD, INC.

Format by the author. Type set in Monotype Bembo by Clarke & Way, Inc. Printed by Colorgraphic Offset Co., Inc.,
New York, on Oxford Sheerwhite. Bound by American Book-Stratford Press, Inc.

To my mother and in memory of my father

ACKNOWLEDGMENTS

I am deeply grateful to the many artists, designers, editors and friends who recommended and loaned treasured books for study and reproduction. The permissions' staffs of the various publishing houses graciously sought and provided the proper acknowledgments. Sue Ellen Curtiss, Sandra Belitza and Deena Pers untiringly assisted in the typing of the manuscript. Michael Horen, Earl l'Abbé, and Virginia Muller made valuable suggestions for the chapter, "The Art and Craft of Illustrating." Clarkson Potter's enthusiasm never waned.

I wish to thank the following publishers and copyright owners for their kindness in allowing me to include the illustrations in this collection:

A. S. BARNES & COMPANY, INC.   Eric Gill: from *The Four Gospels of the Lord Jesus Christ*. Golden Cockerel Press. Waltham Saint Lawrence. 1931.

ERIK BLEGVAD   Water color: from *The* Margaret Rudkin *Pepperidge Farm Cookbook*. ATHENEUM PUBLISHERS. 1963.

JOHN MASON BROWN   Susanne Suba: from *Morning Faces* by John Mason Brown. MCGRAW-HILL BOOK COMPANY. 1949.

CASSELL AND COMPANY, LTD.   E. McKnight Kauffer: from *Elsie and the Child* by Arnold Bennett. 1929.

CROWELL COLLIER AND MACMILLAN, INC.   Anthony Ravielli: from *Relativity for the Million* by Martin Gardner. Text copyright © 1962 by Martin Gardner. Illustrations copyright © 1962 by Anthony Ravielli. THE MACMILLAN COMPANY.

THOMAS Y. CROWELL COMPANY and THE ARTIST   Illustration by Eugene Karlin: from *The Rubaiyat of Omar Khayyam*, copyright © 1964 by THOMAS Y. CROWELL COMPANY.

DELL PUBLISHING CO., INC.   Leonard Baskin: from *The Poppy and Other Deadly Plants* by Esther Baskin. Copyright © 1967 by Leonard and Esther Baskin. A Seymour Lawrence Book. *Delacorte Press.*

FREDERIC DITIS   George Giusti: from *Heart* by George Giusti and Rudolf Hoffman, M.D. © Copyright, 1962, by EDITIONS ALPHA S.A., Geneva, Visual Books.

DOUBLEDAY & COMPANY, INC.   Leonard Baskin: from *The Last Days of Shelley & Byron* by J. E. Morpurgo. ANCHOR BOOKS. 1960; Leonard Baskin: from *People of the Dead Sea Scriptures* by John Marco Allegro. Copyright © 1958 by John Marco Allegro and David Noel Freedman. Reprinted by permission of DOUBLEDAY & COMPANY, INC., and Leonard Baskin; Ludwig Bemelmans: from *Lüchow's German Cookbook* by Jan Mitchell. With an introduction and illustrations by Ludwig Bemelmans. Copyright 1952 by Leonard Jan Mitchell. Reprinted by permission of DOUBLEDAY & COMPANY, INC., and Barrie Books, Ltd.; Thomas Hart Benton: from *The Oregon Trail* by Francis Parkman. Illustrations copyright 1945 by DOUBLEDAY & COMPANY, INC.; Eugene Berman: from *Rome and a Villa* by Eleanor Clark. Copyright 1950, 1951, 1952 by Eleanor Clark. Reprinted by permission of DOUBLEDAY & COMPANY, INC., and Michael Joseph, Ltd.; Warren Chappell: from *The Fairy Ring* edited by Kate Douglas Wiggin and Nora Archibald Smith. Copyright © 1967 by

DOUBLEDAY & COMPANY, INC. Copyright 1906 by MCCLURE, PHILLIPS AND COMPANY; Salvador Dali: from *Essays of Michel de Montaigne*. Selected and illustrated by Salvador Dali. Illustrations copyright, 1947 by DOUBLEDAY & COMPANY, INC.; Hans Erni: from *The Odyssey* by Homer. Translated by Robert Fitzgerald. Copyright © 1961 by Robert Fitzgerald; Betty Fraser: from *I've Got to Talk to Somebody, God* by Marjorie Holmes. Copyright © 1969 by DOUBLEDAY & COMPANY, INC.; Milton Glaser: from *Fierce and Gentle Warriors*. Three stories by Mikhail Sholokhov. Translated by Miriam Morton. Copyright © 1967 by Miriam Morton; David Grose: from *Nature's Year* by John Hay. Copyright © 1961 by John Hay; Antony Groves-Raines: from *Lays of Courtly Love* in verse translation by Patricia Terry. Copyright © 1963 by Patricia Terry; Paul Hogarth: from *Majorca Observed* by Robert Graves and Paul Hogarth. Text copyright © 1954, 1955, 1956, 1957, 1965, by Robert Graves. Illustrations copyright © Paul Hogarth 1965. Used by permission of DOUBLEDAY & COMPANY, INC., and Hope Leresche and Steele; John Langley Howard: from *The Origins of Angling* by John McDonald. Copyright © 1957 by Time Incorporated; Francis Lee Jaques: from *My Wilderness: The Pacific West* by William O. Douglas. Copyright © by William O. Douglas; Robin Jacques: from *The Old Curiosity Shop* by Charles Dickens. A DOLPHIN BOOK; Dong Kingman: from *San Francisco: City on Golden Hills* by Herb Caen and Dong Kingman. Text copyright © 1967 by Herb Caen. Illustrations copyright © 1967 by Dong Kingman; Henry Koerner: from *Tracy's Tiger* by William Saroyan. Copyright 1951 by William Saroyan; Ronald Searle: from *The Anger of Achilles* (Homer's *Iliad*). Translated by Robert Graves. Copyright © 1959 by Robert Graves. Illustrations copyright © 1959 by Ronald Searle. Used by permission of DOUBLEDAY & COMPANY, INC., CASSELL AND COMPANY, LTD., and Hope Leresche and Steele; Judith Shahn: from *Men of the Revolution* by John Tebbel and Ramon Ruiz. Copyright © 1970 by DOUBLEDAY & COMPANY, INC.; Mary Suzuki: from *Amy Vanderbilt's Complete Book of Etiquette*. Copyright 1952, 1954 by Amy Vanderbilt; Charles White: from *Four Took Freedom* by Philip Sterling and Rayford Logan, Ph.D. Copyright © 1967 by DOUBLEDAY & COMPANY, INC.

E. P. DUTTON & CO., INC. Charles Pickard: from *The Call of the Wild* by Jack London. Children's Illustrated Classics Edition. Illustrations copyright © 1968 by J. M. DENT & SONS, LTD.; John Schoenherr: from *Rascal* by Sterling North. Copyright © 1963 by Sterling North. Illustrations copyright © 1963 by E. P. DUTTON & CO., INC.

THE FOLIO SOCIETY, LTD. Edward Bawden: from *Gulliver's Travels* by Jonathan Swift. 1965; Robin Jacques: from *Vanity Fair* by William Makepeace Thackeray. 1963; John Piper: from *The Natural History of Selborne* by Gilbert White. 1962; Leonard Rosoman: from *Point Counter Point* by Aldous Huxley. 1958.

ALAN D. GRUSKIN, MIDTOWN GALLERIES Isabel Bishop: from *Pride and Prejudice* by Jane Austen.

WILLIAM HEINEMANN, LTD. Anthony Gross: from *The Forsyte Saga* by John Galsworthy. Illustrated Edition, 1950.

HILL & WANG, INC. Paul Hogarth: from *A Russian Journey* by Alaric Jacob and Paul Hogarth. Text © Alaric Jacob 1969. Illustrations © Paul Hogarth 1969. Used by permission of HILL & WANG, INC., and CASSELL AND COMPANY, LTD.

HORIZON PRESS John Minton: from *French Country Cooking* by Elizabeth David. © 1951 by Horizon Press; Walter Stein: from *Natural Histories* by Jules Renard. Translated by Richard Howard. Commentary by Edgar Munhall. © 1966 by Horizon Press. *Natural History* by Jules Renard. Lithographs by Walter Stein originally printed by Harvard College Library. Copyright © 1960 by the President and Fellows of Harvard College.

HOUGHTON MIFFLIN COMPANY Victor Ambrus: from *A Glimpse of Eden* by Evelyn Ames. Copyright © 1967 by Evelyn Ames.

ROCKWELL KENT Drawings: from *N by E* by Rockwell Kent. Copyright 1930 by Rockwell Kent.

LITTLE, BROWN AND COMPANY John Alcorn: from *The Abecedarian Book* by Charles W. Ferguson. Copyright

CONTENTS

INTRODUCTION

The art of book illustration is a highly creative process. As in drawing or painting, the artist starts with an idea. It originates with the written word of the author, usually another person but sometimes the artist himself. The artist cogitates on it and has that gift of expression to produce with emotion a story in pictures, a supportive or supplementary embellishment, a decoration or an explanation that makes the text memorable and explicit. Historically beginning with the illuminated manuscript, the storytelling evolved around letters or phrases and then developed into full-page pictures. There are no greater "book" illustrators than Rembrandt and Giotto who took their inspiration from the Bible and painted respectively the famous "Storm on the Sea of Galilee" in oil and the fresco "The Flight into Egypt."

It gives me the greatest pleasure to open a book for the first time and discover, in addition to a page designed for easy reading, illustrations that stimulate my mind and eye. Many readers share my delight. If not, why would there be illustrated books?

Book illustration today is widely if erroneously regarded as a derivative art, an extraneous image forced on the adult reader, costly to commission, prohibitive in price to reproduce in color, and unlikely to increase the sale of a book. Too often, illustration is reserved for children's books, how-to-do-it books, and pocket guides. Nevertheless illustration does help the reader. The English artist Anthony Gross illustrated Galsworthy's *The Forsyte Saga* in 1951; ". . . though this book had never been out of print in thirty years, the Gross edition subsequently sold over fifty thousand copies."*

Book illustration introduces us to the author's world. From there our imagination takes off. The author's tale can be most descriptive but comes alive when the artist fills in the details as when John Tenniel drew what Alice saw on the other side of the looking glass. In *Cream Hill*, Lewis Gannett tells of his children building Midget Village. "They cut windows in the original packaging box, they added an annex. . . ." It is the artist Ruth Gannett who shows us how the completed village looked, its church and belfry, huts and houses, wooden horses and shingle birds. Robert Graves translates in poetry and prose Homer's *Iliad* for *The Anger of Achilles*, but it is Ronald Searle who draws the gods as

* Bob Gill and John Lewis, *Illustrations, Aspects and Directions* (New York, 1964), p. 45.

physical beings, bodily sweeping down from the heavens into action to help us mortals. Once the artist gives a glimpse of the author's world, as in Gustave Doré's illustrations for *The Rime of the Ancient Mariner* or *The Fables of La Fontaine* or Phiz's narrative scenes in *Oliver Twist*, we never forget it. Unfortunately in the past illustrated books were a luxury most adult readers could not afford.

In children's books we share a common visual inheritance. There is Tenniel's Alice, Ernest Shepherd's Mr. Mole, N. C. Wyeth's Long John Silver, Howard Pyle's Robin Hood, Beatrix Potter's Peter·Rabbit. The characterization is powerful, the scene alive, and the detail pertinent. For the adult book the illustration is subtler and just as necessary. The artist, in a role subordinate to the author, creates the character, provides the clothes or costumes, and suggests the setting. In Elizabeth Madox Roberts' *The Time of Man* Clare Leighton does not attempt specific characterization. Instead, we sense the patterns of Ellen Chesser's life in Kentucky, her struggles and hardships and her moments of pleasure. For *San Francisco: City on Golden Hills* Dong Kingman paints the cityscapes as if he had followed author Herb Caen on his jaunts. Representational illustration is extremely effective in books of fantasy. D. W. Dwiggins's people are just right for the H. G. Wells's *The Time Machine*. Henry Koerner's lovers and tiger belong in the New York City of Saroyan's *Tracy's Tiger*.

With the twentieth-century classic the artist paves the way with visual detail for the present picture-conscious generation. Leonard Rosoman recalls the dress of the flappers for Huxley's *Point Counter Point*. In his frontispiece E. McKnight Kauffer symbolizes the milieu of Arnold Bennett's *Elsie and The Child*. For the great books of the past the visual presentation is enlightening. Isabel Bishop, in her character studies for *Pride and Prejudice*, portrays eighteenth-century customs and manners; I would now recognize Jane Austen's Elizabeth Bennett and Lady Catherine de Bourgh immediately. My own introduction to the world of Lilliput was a small watercolor on the jacket of an inexpensive Nelson's Classics edited by Sir Henry Newbolt. Today I feast upon the many illustrations Edward Bawden has contributed to the Folio Society Edition of *Gulliver's Travels*. The most exciting venture in recent English illustration is Bawden's, too.

Early in the nineteen-sixties Edward Bawden conceived the idea of an illustrated Bible. He revealed it to the editors at the Oxford University Press who, it turned out, had been thinking along the same lines. At once they asked Bawden to help plan the project and to take a prominent part in illustrating it. Three volumes of *The Oxford Illustrated Old Testament* appeared in 1968 and two followed in 1969. Twenty-two English artists contributed seven hundred black-

and-white drawings in a variety of mediums. Each artist completed one book or shared a part of a longer book. At the end of each volume, the artists stated their individual principles of illustration and explained how they went about this intellectually demanding assignment. Because of the well-thought-out *mise en pages*, a French term for the placement of all printed material on a book page, the various interpretations in art—storytelling, decorative, and abstract—make an engrossing edition of the Bible. As one reads along, minute triangles in the margins of the page indicate the illustrated passage. I have spent many rewarding hours looking at the illustrations and rereading favorite passages. At the Oxford University Press there is great faith in the importance of the visual aspects of the book. The editors said this succinctly in the catalogue for the exhibition of the Bible drawings held at the Royal Academy of Arts from June 29 to August 11, 1968. "The illustrating of books is an exacting and, at present, an under-regarded art. This exhibition, and the volumes that are to follow, may help to restore the balance." The success of *The Oxford Illustrated Old Testament* lies in the confidence and freedom extended to all the artists who took responsibility in conceptual thinking and applied their excellent graphic skills to the drawings.

The portfolio, *Homage to The Book*, privately published in 1968 by Westvaco, an American corporation, is a fine experiment in making a beautiful book. Fifteen designers including the artists Norman Ives and Joseph Low prepared and edited sample pages which demonstrated how these pages could be "illustrated" with typography, design, drawing, and photography. Paul Rand "illustrated" with type and decorative drawing the third chapter of Genesis, one of the most original presentations. This versatile and talented designer should now be illustrating adult books.

In America and England during the past forty years the illustrated book purchased at the bookshop has flourished as compared to the privately printed, limited edition. Publishers have requested book illustration, editors and art directors have discovered and employed artists, and designers have planned the books with attention and style. I have chosen to examine and study books covering this period from 1929 to 1970 and illustrated by artists of many nationalities. I have made my selections from those I could look at in public libraries and bookshops or through the Limited Editions Club in New York and the Folio Society in London. For this reason I have included *The Poppy and Other Deadly Plants* which Leonard Baskin illustrated magnificently for a commercial publisher rather than *Castle Street Dogs* (1954) or *Horned Beetles and Other Insects* (1957) which he prepared, printed, and distributed at his own Gehenna Press. As important as Baskin's early books are in his development as an illustrator and bookman and as a major influence on young artists, those volumes are limited editions, inaccessible to most readers.

I have intentionally omitted the books illustrated by painters for the collector. It would be unfair to compare the many exceptional fine arts painters with other artists who draw for publication at standard fees and who adapt their skills to mass production. No effort or money was spared when Picasso contributed a flamboyant *Lysistrata* in 1934 for the Limited Editions Club. George Macy, its late president, told of Matisse reading *Ulysses* in one night and, the next morning, outlining his vision of its illustrations which Macy immediately accepted.* The reissue of the illuminated miniature *Jazz* by Matisse in 1960 could only be made available in the United States because it was distributed by the Museum of Modern Art to its members on the occasion of the exhibition of the original plates. Chagall spiritedly illustrated *Burning Lights*, an autobiography of his late wife, Bella Chagall, for Schocken Books in 1946. The current fabulous books of Chagall as well as those of Dali that sell for one thousand dollars and more are not for reading but for the art collector and bibliophile. My selections are restricted to those books that a publisher plans on a realistic budget with the idea that each book must earn its own success. At the beginning of their careers many artists graciously accept meager commissions in return for the joy of illustrating and for the opportunity to make their work known. These artists fill a great need in providing illustrations that all readers can afford and enjoy.

Book Design

Many books are designed as a cohesive unit. The jacket, an important illustration, invites one to open the book. Victor Ambrus accomplished this with an enticing East African landscape in romantic colors for *A Glimpse of Eden* and, inside the book, provided black and white drawings. The binding, decorative endpapers, and title page introduce the visual mood. The late John Minton did this charmingly with the title page for *French Country Cooking*. My interest lies in the sequence of drawings or paintings that reflect, report, and enhance the book. Appearing as frontispieces and, throughout the book, as part titles, full page illustrations, or vignettes within the text, they are drawn in a variety of techniques that require the skill of an artist's eye and hand. There are no photographic illustrations represented because the camera, not the artist, is the eye. The exception is the art of Alexander Alexeïeff whose technique requires a

* *Quarto-Millenary.* New York, 1959. p. 247.

camera in the final stage.

Each example of an illustration is from a bound book designed for reading rather than from a portfolio planned for viewing. The portfolio has advantages. It is frequently larger in size, and its proportions are better suited to drawing than is the oblong shape of most book pages. An artist can set up a press in his studio, experiment with the printing of his work, and assemble the finished sheets as an unbound book. Joseph Low has done just this at his Eden Hill Press. When a book is to contain illustrations in many techniques, it is easier to print each piece of art separately as a single fold, giving individual attention to the quantity of ink needed and, afterwards, to insert the printed pages in a portfolio. The Museum of Modern Art chose this method for Frank O'Hara's *In Memory of My Feelings* (1967) so that the array of illustrations by many artists could be reproduced to perfection. The "book" portfolio is a study in itself. My interest is in the illustrated bound book.

The Artist's Contribution

The artist assumes many roles. He gives the illusion of working simultaneously with the author even though he rarely starts to draw until a manuscript is completed or, with the classics, until centuries have elapsed. He is often a storyteller who recreates a moment or scene and brings the characters to life with an intensity and insight equal to the author's. In this illustrative style he allows his imagination to take up where the author has left off and thereby adds another dimension to the book. Edward A. Wilson's conception of Jules Vernes's *A Journey to the Center of the Earth* is so meticulous and realistic that he leaves no doubt in our minds about the way of life in the earth's interior. We feel that we are a part of the scene. The artist elaborates on the informative and necessary detail of architecture, settings, and clothes. Henry C. Pitz does this exceptionally well as he depicts the soldiers in battles at Crécy and Agincourt for *The Chronicles* of Froissart. With Edward Ardizzoni we attend a nineteenth-century English tea party in Anthony Trollope's *The Warden*. Anthony Gross absorbs the whole of *The Forsyte Saga* and comments on it amply, changing his style with the development of the novel from busy Victorian scenes to sparse vignettes for the later episodes. Leonard Rosoman concentrates on the development of character and evokes the nineteen-twenties in clothes and customs for Huxley's *Point Counter Point*. Henry Koerner takes us to the heart of New York City in 1951 where we identify with the lovers in Saroyan's *Tracy's Tiger*.

Bernarda Bryson likes to share her favorite authors. On her recommendation there is a new edition of Frank R. Stockton's *The Storyteller's Pact* with her finely drawn character studies. David Grose, John Schoenherr, and the late Frances Lee Jaques "follow" the authors on their outdoor jaunts and add the artist's view in storytelling impressions.

The supportive artist does not confine himself to specific incidents. He prefers to synthesize all that the author has said, to convey the essence of the book, and to supplement it in a provocative and rewarding way. Eugene Berman expresses a vast understanding of and an appreciation for Rome in drawings that add visual stature to Eleanor Clark's *Rome and a Villa*. Rockwell Kent symbolizes a philosophical mood in the part-title drawings for his *N by E* in contrast to the storytelling vignettes that dwell upon the trials and joys of his Arctic voyage. John Piper paints his ethereal impressions of Gilbert White's *Selborne*. Independent of Robert Graves, Paul Hogarth reports on the people, the sights, and the countryside for *Majorca Observed*. John Alcorn inveigles us with whimsy and decoration in Charles Ferguson's *The Abecedarian Book*.

The instructive artists have their responsibilities. They explain, inspire, and teach in diagram, design, or representational pictures. After their enthusiasms have developed, they become specialists in a particular field. Their contributions, a necessary part of how-to-do-it books, field guides, and scientific studies, represent a vast amount of correct, meticulous work as seen, for example, in Don Eckleberry's color plates for Richard Pough's *Eastern Land Birds*. I found in *Shorebirds of North America* breathtaking bird paintings by Robert Verity Clem— it was like coming across a beautiful shell on the beach. Exact in detail as to sex, phase, color, and habitat, these studies are a joy to behold and a stimulus to study. It is obvious why the editor for the book, Gardner D. Stout, gratefully acknowledges the artist's work in the introduction. The scholarly and gifted SuZan Noguchi Swain, who favors the biological sciences, helps enlighten Elsie B. Klot's *The New Field Book of Freshwater Life*. George Giusti integrates illustration with text as he designs and paints a fascinating visual sequence about the heart. He breaks away from the conventions of the book and adds a new dimension to anatomical graphics. In recent years the most perceptive illustration for the sciences and social sciences has appeared in the *Scientific American*. Many artists, including Jim Egleson, Thomas Prentiss, Jerome Kuhl, Enid Kotschnig, and Eric Mose, are invaluable contributors to the magazine. Their work should now appear in books.

In my memory there were dozens of cookbooks gaily decorated with nostalgic scenes and useful illustrations. As I went in search of these books, I discovered much careless and uninspired drawing, with one book looking similar to the next. As flattering and intimate as Robert Camp's wash drawings are for Marjorie Kinnan Rawlings's *Cross Creek Cookery* and Sir Francis Rose's pen sketches for *The Alice B. Toklas Cookbook*, they are not excellent examples of draughtmanship nor do they have the verve of the late Ludwig Bemelmans or the solidarity of Edward Bawden, famous for his cookbooks and for *The Week-End Book* (1939). Too few cookbooks include the necessary step-by-step diagrams or recognizable ingredients and utensils. The illustrations should be as explicit as the sequence on how-to-eat a lobster in *Amy Vanderbilt's Complete Book of Etiquette* and as delectable as the ingredients painted by Earl Thollander for James Beard's *Delights and Prejudices*.

This present study of illustration is a sequel to my first book, *The Art of Art for Children's Books*. There I selected an outstanding example from one of several books illustrated by an individual. A budding artist is likely to illustrate two or three children's books a year and as he becomes proficient, he is more daring and expansive. One has only to compare an early Maurice Sendak—*The House of Sixty Fathers* by Miendert Dejong—with his more recent *The Griffin and the Minor Canon* by Frank R. Stockton to realize how completely he has mastered the art of the book.

Of the many artists for children's books, only a few are represented in adult illustration. Editors and publishers tend to think of an artist as belonging to one group or the other, and it is true that certain artists are only for the mature reader. Leonard Baskin does not draw for children. Robert Osborn who has illustrated one juvenile purposely refrains from doing more. The late Ben Shahn readily admitted he could not span both worlds and, with a chuckle, told me he considered *A Boy of Old Prague* an outstanding example of his adult illustration even though the book was published for children. Chatting with Shahn about research for my own book, I told of purchasing an adult Christmas book illustrated by a favorite artist for juvenile publications and being disappointed at finding a repetition of decorations previously used in his juvenile illustration. The artist had not communicated the theme of the adult book. I confessed to Shahn "that I had been took." Shahn suggested I should write this in a letter to the publisher.

Assignments for adult books are scarce and infrequent and the quantity is minute in proportion to the number of books published each year. Certain easel painters, sculptors, and wood engravers—like Leonid, Alexander Calder, Eugene Berman, Charles White, and Clare Leighton—have illustrated but few books. Because of their stature as artists, they look upon the book as another medium of expression and bring to it, even the first time, a perfection in concept and in graphics. Rockwell Kent, Eugene Karlin, Thomas Hart Benton, and the late Reginald Marsh have relished drawing for several books and would have accepted more commissions had they been offered. The prolific illustrators specialize in books and often are equally at ease with adult or juvenile subjects. Edward Ardizzone who has produced hundreds of successful books, can step inside a story and picture it taking place, whether he draws for Thackeray's *Henry Esmond*, Henry Cecil's *Brief to Council*, or his own *Little Tim* books. Robin Jacques, Warren Chappell, Lynd Ward, Bernarda Bryson, and Henry C. Pitz have similar visual powers.

The History of Illustration

The history of illustration is a pursuit in itself and mirrors the path of civilization. It provides a rich commentary on literature and philosophy as well as on customs, clothes, utensils, and architecture. I heartily recommend Philip Bland's *A History of Book Illustration* as a comprehensive study of both eastern and western contributions from "the illuminated manuscript and the printed book," his subtitle, with well-documented reproductions. One can also trace the history of inventions through the making of a book as the craft and technology of printing slowly follows and absorbs the advances in industrialization. The invention of the printing press made possible books with illustrations in quantities never before envisioned. Today electronic scanners help make color reproduction more faithful to the original art. The changes in illustration techniques may be seen in John J. McKendry's excellent *Aesop: Five Centuries of Illustrated Fables* which shows the continuity from a woodcut in 1476 to the etching, the engraving, the wood engraving, and the present-day reproduction of drawings by photo engraving.

Many young artists desire to illustrate a book but they lack experience in the making of a book and do not understand printing and binding procedures. Repeatedly they begin an assignment as if they were making the first and only book. If they have neglected to study what has been done in the past, they cannot continue its traditions or transform a style of a previous era into the present-day manner. Nevertheless, their reluctance not to go back to the past is healthy. The young artists, self-taught or as students, view the masterpieces of art through the ages. They begin to paint or sculpt in imitation of a particular school until they have absorbed and mastered it. Then they emerge as artists in their own right and, with a fresh outlook, produce their idea of a book. However, it is still true that if artists perused illuminated manuscripts, facsimiles of the early books, and reproductions of the outstanding illustrations of the past five hundred years, their own first books would be more rewarding and complete. The late E. McKnight Kauffer's knowledge of the history of book illustration is seen in his treatment of Burton's *The Anatomy of Melancholy*. Robin Jacques continues the tradition of the nineteenth-century French book. Leonard Baskin, equally an originator and a scholar, pursues the art, typography, and printing of a given period and reinterprets its essence in his own idiom. Relevant to the subject are his drawings for John Marco Allegro's *The People of the Dead Sea Scrolls*. Aware of the origins and functions of the *mise en pages*, Warren Chappell meticulously designs as well as illustrates each of his books. It was as a lithographer's apprentice that Ben Shahn learned his skills and craft and, ever afterwards, could prepare his graphics perfectly for reproduction. *The Four Gospels*, illustrated and decorated by the late Eric Gill, was the work of a master who combined the mediaeval with the twentieth century whether he turned his hand to lettering, type design, wood engraving, or sculpture.

The Contemporary Book

The contemporary illustrated book, which has been subjected to many influences from the allied arts and has weathered a variety of trends in design, is emerging in a dramatic and individual way. My collection begins with the nineteen twenties and thirties when the book publisher, who was interested in producing the "beautiful" book, accepted the austere imitation of the private presses. Earlier in America the printer, D. B. Updike, and the book designer, Bruce Rogers, had left their formal mark on the book. They carefully chose their type faces, positioned an artist's illustrations to fit into their over-all design, demanded excellent paper, and supervised the presswork. The artist benefited when his illustrations appeared in the handsomely solid books printed by the Lakeside Press in Chicago and the Merrymount Press in Cambridge, Massachusetts. In England the Nonesuch, Golden Cockerel, and Curwen Presses produced equally fine books. T. M. Cleland and W. A. Dwiggins, two leading American book designers in the nineteen twenties, added freedom and flair to the tales they illustrated. Dwiggins' treatment of H. G. Wells's *The Time Machine* is the work of a total book artist. Dwiggins devised the *mise en pages*, created illustrations in a stencil technique, and had the text set in a type face he had designed. It was in 1929 that the young Lynd Ward created in woodcut *Gods' Man*, a novel without words, as exciting an experiment as any book being made today. S. A. Jacobs, the witty and volatile typographer of the Golden Eagle Press, coordinated Alexander Calder's drawings with the verse so perfectly that *Three Young Rats and Other Rhymes* was a jewel. There were artists who were able to control every detail of the *mise en pages* even though they were only responsible for the illustrations. Rockwell Kent did just that with his *N by E*. Lynton Lamb worked in this manner with the Oxford University Press in England.

The Influence of World War II

World War II with its restrictions was responsible for changes in the style and mood of book design. The powerful influence of the designer-printer dwindled as the publisher had to assume control over bookmaking and the quantity of paper used. Paper was of an inferior grade which would not last one hundred years even with the best of care. Staff book designers kept the text page as small as possible to save material and labor. With these restrictions the artist could not be given proper attention or freedom to experiment. Richard Lindner, who completed an abundance of illustrations for *Tales from Hoffmann* edited by Christopher Lazare in 1946, found his art not reproduced to his liking. Even today Mr. Lindner is unhappy about this book, and for this very reason, an illustration from it is not in my collection. He considers it pointless to draw for books printed on inferior paper and trimmed to an inadequate size. I understand his disappointment and mention it because his illustrations, pertinent in content and masterfully delicate, contribute immensely to the stories and are important in any study of illustration. He uses his talent in other directions—a great loss to the book world.

Even if paper and printing are mediocre, art can give visual pleasure and add meaning and depth to the storytelling. In the nineteen-forties I came across three paperback treasures, new editions of G. B. Shaw's *Pygmalion* illustrated by Feliks Topolski, Elizabeth David's *French Country Cooking* with drawings by John Minton, and William Saroyan's *My Name is Aram* illustrated by Don Freeman. I bought them as much for the art as the contents and have them in my library till this day.

In spite of wartime restrictions fine books continued to appear. The catalogues of the Fifty Books of the Year exhibitions sponsored by the American

Institute of Graphic Arts report and show distinguished work accomplished with limited materials by the book designers. Some of these books should be considered for reprinting today. Toward the end of the war Doubleday initiated the Doubleday Limited Editions and made it possible for the outstanding easel painters in America to illustrate in color and in drawing. Thomas Hart Benton produced a warm and romantic interpretation of Francis Parkman's *The Oregon Trail* and Salvador Dali added a biting commentary to *Essays of Michel de Montaigne*.

Two noteworthy trends are apparent in the late nineteen-forties and fifties. One is humorous non-fiction affectionately illustrated by artists famous for their drawings in *The New Yorker* or their impressions and caricatures in the New York *Times* and the once influential New York *Herald Tribune*. These experienced artists, who thrived on interpreting the written word, had made hundreds of drawings to the required proportions. They were not daunted by the reproductive process or the meeting of deadlines. To appreciate their insights and to view their excellence in anatomy and perspective, one has only to glance at the drawings by Carl Rose for C. B. Palmer's *Slightly Cooler in the Suburbs* and Jean Kerr's *Please Don't Eat the Daisies* and those of Gluyas Williams, Whitney Darrow, Jr., and R. Taylor for Corey Ford's *Has Anybody Seen Me Lately?* My collection shows the charming study in reminiscence by Susanne Suba for John Mason Brown's *Morning Faces*.

The second important development, continuing to the present day, is the change taking place in supportive and supplementary illustration. Marvin Bileck showed promise of brilliant mood illustration in Alfred Kazin's *A Walker in the City* (1951). Why didn't the art director have Bileck work on a larger scale? Why wasn't Bileck given more assignments along these lines so that he could develop his style? Fortunately, his whimsy and fantasy have been discovered for children's books.

One needs years of experience in drawing and painting to crystallize a style of illustration that often blends realism with abstraction. Matisse, after a lifetime of painting, started experimenting with collage in 1939. At the suggestion of the French publisher E. Teriade, in 1942 Matisse combined collage with his handwriting to make a harmonious balance of art and text for the book which finally emerged as *Jazz* in 1947. Wisely, editors did not commission this illustrative approach at random. Paul Rand, in his book design for Thomas Mann's *Tables of the Law* and Nicholas Monsarrat's *Leave Cancelled*, handled it maturely by typography alone.

The Present Freedom in Illustration

What brought about the new freedom in book illustration was the success of children's picture books where the increased use of offset printing economically permitted the artist to paint in black wash or in watercolor over the entire page and to integrate the text with the art. The artist and publisher observed these experiments in children's books. Adults often bought the books for themselves. Robert Osborn, who always understood the blending of type and illustration, brought it to perfection in *Osborn on Leisure* (1956). The painter Joseph Albers translated his thinking into line for his *Poems and Drawings* (1958). Antonio Frasconi made his first picture stories for children and then envisioned adult subjects which he published himself or at E. Weyhe, Inc., and the Museum of Modern Art. Harcourt, Brace & World published his brilliant rendering of *Bestiary/Bestiario* by Pablo Neruda. Without offset printing Paul Hogarth might never have been allowed to work in watercolor for Alaric Jacob's *Russian Journey* and Dong Kingman's paintings might have appeared only in art books rather than as an accompaniment to Herb Caen's *San Francisco: City on Golden Hills*.

An artist's work is no longer poorly reproduced. If he is not knowledgeable about type faces and the *mise en pages*, there are many dedicated book designers to help him today. At Atheneum the book designer Harry Ford, who is devoted to producing exceptional books, is responsible for the attractive settings for Earl Thollander's paintings in *Delights and Prejudices* and for Eric Blegvad's decorations in *The* Margaret Rudkin *Pepperidge Farm Cookbook*.

I have not discussed or included unsuccessful book illustration because the fault was not always or solely the artist's. It was also the responsibility of the entire publishing staff, the printer, and even the binder. I have presented those excellent illustrations for which the artist has given generously of his creativeness and the publishing house has allowed him freedom of expression and provided the best reproduction within its budget and bookmaking standards.

Each selection, in the pages that follow, represents an individual book. A single reproduction does not take the place of an entire book but it gives one a chance to see treasures that one might otherwise not know existed.

AUTHOR'S NOTE ABOUT THE ILLUSTRATIONS

Beneath the illustration the artist is identified first, then the book title, the medium used, the book size, and the year of publication. The illustration should be enjoyed regardless of medium although it controls and influences what the artist does. The width precedes the height in the book size. A dotted line around the art indicates the proportions of the page to help one visualize the limited area in which the artist has worked.

If the artist could use any medium and were allowed a full palette of color, all books would be extraordinarily beautiful. Given specifications for an assignment, one artist will handle the same medium quite differently from another. For this reason I offer brief explanations of the various mediums. A line drawing means a drawing in line of varying thicknesses without gradations of tone and including, perhaps, solid black areas. A woodcut is a line drawing cut on wood. The effect is coarser than that of the wood engraving where the most delicate line can be engraved on the hard end grain of the wood block. A wash drawing, made with a brush, shows gradations of tone. As in a pencil drawing, the tones vary from pure black to the palest grey to allow soft and subtle shading. For line or wash drawings in color separation the artist prepares a key drawing in black and draws the other colors on separate overlays in register with the key plate. An artist makes a lithograph by drawing with a grease crayon on the grained surface of a stone and proving that drawing on stone on a paper surface. He might work in black only, or if he wishes color, he draws each color on a separate stone, and in proving them, makes a print in full color. A watercolor is a painting done with a complete palette of watercolors, tempera, or gouache.

The Storytellers

ALEXANDER ALEXEÏEFF

VICTOR AMBRUS

EDWARD ARDIZZONE

EDWARD BAWDEN *(see color section)*

LEONARD BASKIN

LUDWIG BEMELMANS

THOMAS HART BENTON

ISABEL BISHOP

ERIK BLEGVAD *(see color section)*

BERNARDA BRYSON

MIGUEL COVARRUBIAS

ALEXANDER CALDER

WARREN CHAPPELL

HANS ERNI

SALVADOR DALI *(see color section)*

W. A. DWIGGINS

RUTH GANNETT

DOMENICO GNOLI

DAVID GROSE

ANTHONY GROSS

ANTONY GROVES-RAINES

FRANCIS HOYLAND

FRANCIS LEE JAQUES

ROBIN JACQUES

FRITZ KREDEL

E. MCKNIGHT KAUFFER *(see color section)*

ROCKWELL KENT

HENRY KOERNER

LYNTON LAMB

DAVID LEVINE

ROBERT OSBORN *(see color section)*

CHARLES PICKARD

HENRY C. PITZ

PHILIP REISMAN

BRIAN ROBB

LEONARD ROSOMAN

CYRIL SATORSKY

JOHN SCHOENHERR

SUSANNE SUBA

RONALD SEARLE

BEN SHAHN

MARC SIMONT

FELIKS TOPOLSKI

LYND WARD

CAREL WEIGHT

BRIAN WILDSMITH

N. C. WYETH

EDWARD A. WILSON

ALEXANDER ALEXEÏEFF
Doctor Zhivago,
screen of pins and photography,
6½ × 9⅜ inches, 1958

Fascinating, somber, and the embodiment of everything Russian, Alexeïeff's illustration borrows from the art of the film. Single scenes alternate with sequences wherein people and action change gradually, the pace of the story evolves, and the landscapes and interiors of Russia emerge. As Boris Pasternak himself wrote: "It is the spirit of the book that Alexeïeff has rendered. Everything in it that was composed or mysterious is grasped and conceived marvelously."

A technique other than drawing succeeds when the artist can control it as readily as his pen. Alexeïeff does this with the camera. Instead of the camera being the eye, he selects what to shoot. First he makes a scene in relief from a pattern of steel pins set in a three by four foot white plastic screen. Then he casts an oblique beam of light on the shadow picture and photographs it as an illustration. For a sequence he changes the position of the pins to show further action or other characters.

Alexeïeff's recent illustrations for Dostoyevsky's *Notes from the Underground* and *The Gambler* have a refinement and clarity missing from *Doctor Zhivago*. Of greater importance is that this artist could capture the essence of a contemporary novel as well as those stories already in his heritage.

VICTOR AMBRUS *A Glimpse of Eden*, line drawings, 5½ × 8¼ inches, 1967

A gifted illustrator for adults or children, Victor Ambrus listens to the text until he has the exact picture. He discovers the splendor of the leopard "lying flung across the log," the silkiness of his pelt, his arrogance and voluptuousness. Ambrus made study after study at the London zoo. The final drawings he did in his studio. Landscapes without figures are deadly dull to him, while people and animals are of equal importance. Throughout *A Glimpse of Eden* he captures their majestic qualities as seen in the East Africa Highland. His line studies highlight one dominant figure or animal with a suggestion of scenery. One would like to see repeated as frontispiece paintings his jacket scenes with their changing color from sunshine to shadow over figures and landscape. These beautiful jackets, including the one for Evelyn Ames' *A Glimpse of Eden*, are soon to be lost forever.

VII

WHEN NJOROGI SCRATCHED on our tent next morning, the full moon still hung like a lamp in the acacia branches and only a narrow stroke of hibiscus pink brushed the dark eastern horizon: we were after leopards and wanted to be out hunting by daybreak. They are the shyest of animals, increasingly so as more women wear their coats, and many travelers go home without having seen even one. Sometimes, however, you may find one lying in the early morning sun at the edge of the bush before he hides up for the day, or in the branches of a tree where he may have dragged a kill and stuffed it into a crotch, or running between bushes in a rough little glade. Even when in plain sight leopards can

EDWARD ARDIZZONE   *The Warden*, line drawings, 5 × 8 inches, 1952

The effervescent Mr. Ardizzone emphatically agrees adult books should be
illustrated. Over a long career he has handled at least sixty adult books and, when
you include his children's books, the number of drawings and watercolors run
into the thousands. Whether he is illustrating a classic or writing and sketching
his World War II diaries, *Baggage to the Enemy*, he brings all his life and soul
to an assignment. He likes to think about the book and live with it awhile. Then
he creates the scene with emphasis on personalities against the detail of an
authentic setting—here the intrigue of the Warden's tea party about to begin
with the young ladies shyly awaiting the young gentlemen, the elderly gentlemen merely chatting while the ornately dressed elderly lady watches the
proceedings. The whole world of Trollope comes alive as Ardizzone adds to the
description. Keenly aware of the proportions of the book page, he gets the
complete scene in. Ever considerate of reproduction methods Ardizzone lavishly
illustrates with ample shading in line for letterpress or with touches of wash
for offset.

   A fine watercolorist, well represented in museum collections, he considers it an
honor and a delight to contribute to the book. Ardizzone has favorites and lists
among his best *Henry Esmond* (Limited Editions Club), *Robinson Crusoe* (The
Nonesuch Press), and the contemporary volumes *A Stickful of Nonpareil* by
George Scurfield and *Brief to Council* by Henry Cecil. For *The Oxford Illustrated
Old Testament* he recently illustrated I Samuel, Jonah, and the second half of
Ecclesiasticus with his usual insight—when to convey the poetic drama, the
teachings, or the humor.

LEONARD BASKIN   *The People of the Dead Sea Scrolls* in Text and Pictures,
line drawings, 7 × 10¼ inches, 1958

Baskin is known primarily for his sculpture and printmaking. He is also dedicated to the art and
the craft of the total book. As early as 1942 and starting earnestly in 1951, Leonard Baskin both
accepted and broke away from traditional bookmaking to illustrate, set, print, bind, and publish
books as a personal experience under his private Gehenna Press imprint. From these years of
experiment came a contribution that enriched the trade book—the portfolio *Voyages* by Hart
Crane, the *Iliad of Homer*, *Creatures of Darkness*, *The Poppy and Other Deadly Plants*, and *The
Divine Comedy*.

   In 1957 Leonard Baskin enthusiastically drew eleven illustrations for *The People of the Dead Sea
Scrolls*. In his drawings, he evoked the spirit of the past to contrast with the realistic photographs
of the archaeological excavations of the ancient Qumran Essenic community taken by the author,
John Marco Allegro. Baskin, a former student for the rabbinate, told us how the Essenes, an ascetic
Jewish philosophical sect that existed at the time of Christ, lived, ate, dressed, and worshiped.
In strong line well-accented with blacks, his picture of their religious communal meal conveyed
the ritual of this moment in their daily life. The author was greatly annoyed at the artist's
imaginative interpretation and demanded that the eleven drawings remain unpublished. That
decision leaves the reader poorer.

LEONARD BASKIN *The Poppy and Other Deadly Plants,*
line drawings, 8¼ × 11 inches, 1967

Of Leonard Baskin's illustration, no example is typical and each is outstanding because he adapts his work to what is at one with the subject. Not only is *The Poppy and Other Deadly Plants* a book of extraordinary beauty that haunts one's memory, it is also a knowledgeable collection of nature drawings. One senses the relationships in a perfect book. Nineteen drawings were not done in one graphic style to fill a preconceived design. Rather each plant lives and grows in its own manner on a full page and provides the design of the page in contrast to the classic typography of the facing text. Baskin fully understands gravure printing and he, being the master of this process, uses the heaviest blacks, the finest shading, and the thinnest of pen lines to capture the detail and the texture.

Botanically correct, the hemlock, the jack-in-the-pulpit, the passion flower, or the entire poppy plant encompass the history, folklore, and superstition of the text. Here this single poppy, paper-thin, dazzles in its rich use of black on white and entices one into the sinister magic of its heart.

LUDWIG BEMELMANS
Lüchow's German Cookbook,
line drawings,
5¼ × 7⅞ inches, 1952

Whether Bemelmans was illustrating his personal histories like *I Love You, I Love You, I Love You* or this cookbook, his sense of humor and observation of people's moods were evident. His line style was quick and facile. He decorated an entire drawing in such a way that one could join the scene at Lüchow's, share the philandering and mischief, and sniff the bouquet of wines along with the aroma of cigars. In the smaller drawings he sometimes dashed off a few tempting ingredients. Purposely, he made no pretense at explaining cooking methods. Through the artist's love of people, intimate moments, small scenes, fun and discomforts, one is encouraged to try the recipes and to make the "gemütlich" of Lüchow's at home.

When Bemelmans used color, a line drawing was the basis of the painting, the palette was joyful and vibrant, and the effect was that of a mural bustling with exuberance.

THOMAS HART BENTON *The Oregon Trail*, watercolor, 6⅝ × 9½ inches, 1945

The Missouri-born painter Thomas Hart Benton is proud of his America and celebrates its people, the glories of its land, and its adventures in history. The vitality and expansive style he uses at the easel, he carries forth in the book, composing a historical scene as if it were happening today. A report rather than a commentary, this is his re-creation of how a frontier post looked in 1846, with the Indians in their red and blue blankets and brass earrings swarming around the shrewd trader.

His watercolors, sunny and folksy, lyrical and rhythmic, cover every phase of life on the trail. There are the hardships—the pioneers heroically struggling on mules over rocky terrain and against thunderstorms. Benton is equally adept at presenting Indian folklore and paints the superstition of thunder as a great black bird swooping down and brandishing lightning. In contrast he captures the moments of inaction and freedom from peril when the trappers, men of individuality and character, encamp with friends and swap tall tales. Whenever possible Benton fits into the scenes the majesty of the landscape with its wild flowers, roaming animals, and glorious plains against the distant, overshadowing Black Hills and enormous color-streaked skies.

ISABEL BISHOP *Pride and Prejudice*, sketch for wash drawing (unpublished)
5⅜ × 8½ inches (size of sketch)

The selection of Isabel Bishop as illustrator for *Pride and Prejudice* was an unusual and perceptive one. In the nineteen-fifties Isabel Bishop immersed herself in Jane Austen's world and brought her characters to life with the intensity, the elegance of line, and the mastery of costume that she uses for her genre studies of the New York City scene. Because she handles space and light in the tradition of the Old Masters, her figures in authentic English Regency dress are solid and active without benefit of scenery or interiors. She does several versions of a drawing, each of which could be the final one. In this particular study we are aware of Lady Catherine de Bourgh's anger toward Elizabeth Bennet, "I send no compliments to your mother." We also see Elizabeth as a match for the haughtiness and arrogance of Lady Catherine. That these drawings remain unpublished is one of the aggravations and disappointments shared by the artist, Jane Austen fans, and all readers.

BERNARDA BRYSON
The Storyteller's Pack,
line drawings,
6⅝ × 9⅛ inches, 1968

Sometimes the finest book illustration
occurs when an artist has read and
adored an author's work from child-
hood. Frank Stockton's tales have been
in Bernarda Bryson's imagination since
then and the scenes she chooses tell the
point of each story in this collection.
She captures the characters of the two
competent Kansas homemakers, with
their straight hair drawn tightly back
into a bun. When disaster besets them in
the midst of a cruise, they face the
situation with the same practicality they
used in housewifery. One brings along a
canoe paddle in the story, "The Casting
Away of Mrs. Lecks and Mrs. Aleshine."

You never forget the impression of a
Bernarda Bryson scene intently done
with sympathy and a sense of humor.
She establishes character and setting in a
firm line and weaves in a pattern of
decoration to highlight the mood of an
episode. In the drawing here, the waves
actually swish and swirl around the two
ladies under a lowering sky.

In the nineteen-forties and nineteen-
fifties Miss Bryson enriched the pages of
Scientific American, *Fortune*, and *Harper's*
with an artistry not often found in
magazine illustration. Now, in her work
as book illustrator, she takes it upon
herself to rediscover long-forgotten
books such as Frank R. Stockton's.
Or she researches and tells in her own
words the ancient Near Eastern epic of
the legendary hero-king *Gilgamesh* and
sympathetically works with the designer
on the *mise en pages*.

MIGUEL COVARRUBIAS
Mexico South,
watercolor, line drawings,
photographs, 6¼ × 9⅜ inches, 1946

Miguel Covarrubias was a man of flair
and immeasurable talent. Well-known
as a painter and caricaturist, he traveled
the world to study the life and art of
primitive peoples and afterwards expertly
wrote and illustrated books about their
civilizations.

Mexico South typified his versatility.
Covarrubias, whenever the text demands,
gave every detail of the culture of the
Isthmus of Tehuantepec in lively line
scenes, caricature portraits, Rousseau-
like paintings, stippled renderings of
archaeological diggings, animated maps,
and diagrams of art motifs, fabric designs,
and floor plans. The frontispiece of the
river scene, no mere decoration, is a
beautiful combination of present and
past in lush and glowing color. Even
today one sees the same kind of mon-
umental native woman as she glides along
with her market basket on her head while
the ruffle of her skirt flutters gracefully.
The low rolling hills and the rich green-
lands come down to the river's edge
where formerly the women bathed
unselfconsciously in the muddy waters.

No appreciation of Covarrubias would
be complete without examining the
illustrations for his *Island of Bali,* his *The
Eagle, the Jaguar & the Serpent,* Hudson's
Green Mansions, and a fabulous, flamboyant interpretation in dragon-like colors
of a Chinese classic, *All Men Are Brothers.*

UP in the North, a long way off,
The donkey's got the whooping cough.

ALEXANDER CALDER   *Three Young Rats and Other Rhymes*, line drawings,
7½ × 10 inches, 1946

A mobile is a drawing in space with a potential of animation. Magically Alexander Calder
transfers this concept of sculpture to drawings on the printed page. Turn the donkey's tail and he
raises his head. Or spin the wheel and the three mice card and gather the wool. Mother Goose
rhymes are not only for children, and Alexander Calder has no inhibitions about illustrating them
with realism and wit for his own delight. If the verse says, "three little mice sit down to spin,"

THREE little mice sat down to spin.
Pussy passed by and she peeped in.
"What are you at, my fine little men?"
"Making coats for gentlemen."
"Shall I come in and cut off your threads?"
"Oh no, Mistress Pussy, you'd bite off our heads!"

49

the artist draws the very action, and adds a ravenous sneer to Mistress Pussy.

As early as 1931 when his wire sculptures were exhibited in Paris, he illustrated in this strong, "mobile" line style his first book, the *Fables of Aesop*. There is an added excellence to *Three Young Rats* and the more recent *A Bestiary* because the master book designers S. A. Jacobs and Joe Blumenthal understood the need of space around Calder's drawings and handled it as an integral part of the *mise en pages*.

48

themselves so. The truth was, the nation as a body was in the world for one object, and one only: to grovel before king and Church and noble; to slave for them, sweat blood for them, starve that they might be fed, work that they might play, drink

misery to the dregs that they might be happy, go naked that they might wear silks and jewels, pay taxes that they might be spared from paying them, be familiar all their lives with the degrading language and postures of adulation that they might walk in pride and think themselves the gods of this world. And for all this, the thanks they got were cuffs and contempt; and

WARREN CHAPPELL

A Connecticut Yankee in King Arthur's Court, line drawings, 6¼ × 9½ inches, 1942

Warren Chappell can draw people and animals, interiors and landscape, or furnishings and fabrics. He conveys action, repose, humor, and tragedy as he tells a story, adds to it, or decorates it. A book designer, calligrapher, and typographer, he understands book format, does not try to go beyond its conventions, and overlooks no detail. The illustration, in live, strong line or rich, lusty watercolor, runs alongside its text, so that you are not groping for it, and fits within the type area. The binding, in pure and brilliant color, becomes a decorative cloak that reflects the spirit of the volume for The Heritage Press.

Chappell is a perfect choice to illustrate Mark Twain's writings. He matches the author's energy, invention, imagination, and verve. A realist who speaks out for causes but adores fantasy, he can poke fun along with Mark Twain at pomposity, oppression, or superstition. He can draw an idea. What wittier interpretation of this medieval tale and what greater satire of chivalry can there be than this scene with the poor literally supporting the church and the nobility in all their luxury?

Equally individual and superb are Chappell's illustrations for *The History of Tom Jones*, *Tragedies of Shakespeare*, *Blue Trout and Black Truffles* by Joseph Wechsberg, and *Come Hither* by Walter de la Mare. If only there were many other artists to do books as well Chappell does his!

HANS ERNI
The Odyssey,
line drawings,
6⅛ × 9¼ inches, 1961

It takes vision and experience in drawing to match the inspiration and scope of the twenty-four books of this epic. Hans Erni has these gifts and uses them in his mercurial and elegant style to convey the beauty we associate with ancient Greece. Rightly for *The Odyssey*, Erni makes no attempt at specific character and leaves the settings vague for us to imagine the barbaric splendor of the palaces of the Mycenaean period. He includes chariots, ships, and spears when necessary for the travel adventures. Each drawing is the essence of a dramatic episode or a touching moment. From Book Three, here is both the spirit and brutality in a ritual offering to the gods. The heifer with all his might struggles valiantly while (astride him) a son of Hector subdues him and another son stands ready "for the stroke of sacrifice."

The lines flow from Erni's pen with spontaneity and freedom. Drawn in the merest detail the facial expressions reflect concern, passion, grief, and tenderness as the heroes and gods, warriors and helmsmen, elders and children, soaring eagles, savage wolves, and sleeping dogs take part in the saga.

Absorbed and exacting in his research, Hans Erni has expressed himself successfully in many graphic mediums—stage designs, murals, ceramics, posters, institutional advertisements, magazine covers, portraits, and books including *Marcus Aurelius, The Meditations,* and the colorful volumes of the Doubleday Pictorial Library on Science and Nature.

W. A. DWIGGINS   *The Time Machine*, stencil in color separation, 6 × 9⅛ inches, 1931

In Dwiggins' words illustrations are called for "when they can make a stage setting for the story. When they ornament it or suggest it, perhaps, instead of reveal it." In this eerie scene, with just one shade of azure blue, Dwiggins creates a mood of expectation for the impending dramatic moment as The Time Traveller seeks shelter from the heat and glare and hastens into the colossal ruin that H. G. Wells described.

Dwiggins was one of the few illustrators who understood ornament and had the gift of composing his own for emphasis, sometimes exuberantly and always with variety and grace. For this scene, he designed an olive and turquoise border like a door opening upon the vast view. He planned every detail of the book from the choice of type face to the *mise en pages* and stenciled

the pictures and ornaments so that they would have a closer affinity to letter forms than a line drawing. He used no black and obtained different moods by combining three or four muted shades from a nine-color palette.

An inquisitive traditionalist, a writer, a designer of type faces, a letterer and a puppeteer, Dwiggins stamped his personality on the entire book, and, when necessary, with mischief and merriment. The study of the art of the book would be incomplete without a perusal of some of the hundreds of books he designed and ornamented or without reading his essays collected in *MSS.*, published in 1947 as a book. Right now his work is not fashionable; hopefully it will come into favor again.

RUTH GANNETT
Cream Hill:
Discoveries of a Weekend Countryman,
lithographs,
5⅝ × 8⅜ inches, 1945

The charm of Ruth Gannett lies in her ability to share the intimate knowledge of her world with us. Clearly and precisely, in the soft texture of the lithograph, she draws the midget village built by her children inside the barn: a church with a belfry among the houses, wooden horses, shingle-birds, and a view of the Connecticut countryside. Other studies include their living room, the old schoolhouse, the favorite wild plants—skunk cabbage, mandrake, and ostrich ferns— and for the endpapers a picture plan of the entire village, all perfectly appropriate for her husband Lewis Gannett's book on country living.

DOMENICO GNOLI

A Journal of the Plague Year &c. 1665,
line drawings and
watercolor,
7⅛ × 10⅜ inches, 1968

Defoe's journal is a documentary novel
to which Gnoli's vivid imagination
blends fantasy with authentic visual
detail. He leaves no doubt in the reader's
mind that this is the way the people of
London lived, looked, and acted in the
dreadful year of 1665. Gnoli effortlessly
creates haunting, eerie scenes that do not
spare the reader from the atrocities or
horrors. A talented painter, he is extremely dramatic in the manipulation of light
on color and in the execution of unusual
perspectives. Also a stage designer, he
understands the need for surprise and
exaggeration. His eight paintings for the
Limited Editions Club volume are akin
to those breath-taking moments at the
theatre when the curtain is raised on a
distinctive setting with the characters
unobtrusively taking part in a scene such
as pictured in this rebuilding of "an old
decay'd house."

   In 1961 Gnoli wrote and illustrated the
beguiling fairy tale, *Orestes, or the Art of
Smiling*. Earlier he designed sets for
As You Like It and *The Merchant of Venice*
and contributed a fanciful portfolio of
drawings, "Cities of Italy," to *Horizon*.
His paintings are in the permanent
collections of many museums.

DAVID GROSE   *Nature's Year*, wood engravings, 5½ × 8¼ inches, 1961

David Grose is a naturalist whose wood engraving impressions of his adopted Cape Cod are unforgettable in John Hay's three books, *Nature's Year*, *The Run*, and *The Great Beach*. Grose exults in showing us the streams, coves, dunes, and wildlife in the warmth of new spring, at the height of summer, and in desolate autumn, so beautifully described by John Hay. Alewives skitter in the ponds, gulls circle overhead, little holes made by the sand hoppers are seen along the empty stretches of beach, sunlight plays on the stained shingles of the old mill, and—in *Nature's Year* during November—the grasshopper jumps along a stalk of wild grass. Wood engraving is a medium that allows delicate detail which David Grose discerningly uses to its fullest extent.

ANTHONY GROSS   *The Forsyte Saga*, line drawings and lithographs in color separation,
6⅝ × 9⅛ inches, 1950

If twentieth-century classics are to be illustrated, let them be done with the verve and abundance
of Anthony Gross. Twenty-six drawings, numerous vignettes, and twelve glowing lithographs
capture the Forsyte "age and way of life" convincingly described by John Galsworthy. Beginning
with 1886, Anthony Gross shows the large family gatherings at festive teas, dinner parties, and
private balls under crystal chandeliers and amid potted palms. The scenes change with the passing
of the Victorian era to simpler individual encounters set against nostalgic backdrops of country
houses, London streets, and Paris views until finally in 1920, the story ends.

In line as delicate as lace and then in bold brush strokes Anthony Gross elaborates every nuance.
One is aware of streaming sunshine, gentle spring evenings, and the melancholy of fast-falling
leaves in October as the well-groomed men of property, the captivating women, and the
capricious youth take their parts in the saga. He has the gift of choosing the pivotal scene, as
above, and reporting it as if he had been there. One sees the stylish Irene, the architect Bosinney,
and the fur-coated Swithin view with rapt interest the building of the "Fatal House" at
Robin Hill.

The artist composes his color plates in black line and with the eye of a painter he so mixes, on
separate overlays, lemon-yellow, orange, pearl-grey, the peach hue of dawn, and a soft, cheerful
blue that the colors radiate moods of celebration or introspection.

ANTONY GROVES-RAINES
Lays of Courtly Love,
line drawings,
4³⁄₁₆ × 7⅛ inches, 1963

Evocative and romantic, the six drawings
of Antony Groves-Raines grace this
small book with the exquisiteness of
miniatures. Within the narrow shape of
the page the artist fits scenes of twelfth-
century romances. Realizing that black
does not print solidly in rubber plate
printing, Antony Groves-Raines turns
this to his advantage. His drawings are
like engravings in brass. The small areas
of black have a worn, rubbed look. With
his intricate use of decoration he gives
the impression of rich embroidered silks
in the Norman fashion. The scenes of joy
and sadness take place in front of stylized
settings of the tile roofs and carved stone
capitals of chapels and castles.

Every detail is relevant to the ritual of
courtly love for the frontispiece of
"Eliduc," shown here. The weasel has
just brought her own mate back from the
hold of Death by placing a crimson
flower inside his mouth. Now with the
same flower the devoted wife of Eliduc
is going to save the life of the beautiful,
pale maiden Eliduc loves.

Educated at Cambridge, Antony
Groves-Raines delights in exacting
research and absorbs and digests the
material until he is able to present it in
a new light. Particularly fond of and
skillful in the art of *trompe l'œil*, he
turned to this style for the enchanting
watercolors in John Langstaff's *On
Christmas Day in the Morning!*

FRANCIS HOYLAND
II Samuel, wash drawings,
5¾ × 9¼ inches, 1968

The Book of II Samuel continues the
narrative of David, the warrior and poet,
who had an unshakable faith in the Lord.
To quote the artist, Hoyland vividly
experiences "the deepening mood of
tragedy enveloping David" and conveys
this with deep reverence in twenty-four
dramatic wash drawings, one for each
chapter, in *The Oxford Illustrated Old
Testament*.

Surprisingly Hoyland works in
relatively small areas, from quarter page
to three-quarter page, and his use of
black wash overpainted with black line
has a richness found only in full color
painting together with an interplay of
light and shadow in the tradition of the
Old Masters. Here, for II Samuel 6, he
interprets the historical details of how
David might have looked in his
liturgical garment and how the Ark
might have been built with the two
cherubim atop it, composite beings
facing each other in the traditional
ancient Near Eastern, heraldic manner.
In the foreground David is spiritedly
leaping and dancing before the Lord in a
desire to serve him.

Francis Hoyland is reflective and
versatile. Faced with illustrating Deuter-
onomy for Oxford, he turns to "simple,
abstract drawings" more fitting for this
book of Mosaic law than for the direct
and violent expressions of II Samuel.

2 SAMUEL 6

come to me?" So David would not remove the ark of the Lord unto him into the city of David: but David carried it aside into the house of Obed-edom the Gittite. And the ark of the Lord continued in the house of Obed-edom the Gittite three months: and the Lord blessed Obed-edom, and all his household. And it was told king David, saying, "The Lord hath blessed the house of Obed-edom, and all that pertaineth unto him, because of the ark of God." So David went and brought up the ark of God from the house of Obed-edom into the city of David with gladness. And it was so, that when they that bare the ark of the Lord had gone six paces, he sacrificed oxen and fatlings. And David danced before the Lord with all his might; and David was girded with a linen

FRANCIS LEE JAQUES *My Wilderness*, line drawings, 6 × 9⅛ inches, 1960

These drawings convey the reverence and wonderment for the Pacific West that permeate William O. Douglas's *My Wilderness*. There is tranquillity and natural beauty all around. At forty-five hundred feet while climbing Mount Adams, Justice Douglas probably saw this very scene of rams and ewes pausing as they grazed on the rugged terrain. The clear coldness of Adams Lake is evident from the shimmering reflection in its waters.

Jaques was an outstanding naturalist who understood the relationship of flora and fauna and created each scene as a three-dimensional study, with feeling and appreciation. In chiseled black line and with discipline he drew the forest floor of the Olympic range with its carpets of fungi and ferns and its herds of deer. Or he depicted winter fishing for steelheads in pools shaded by towering western hemlocks. He reproduced the majestic vistas of the snow-crowned peaks of the high sierras.

Jaques traveled extensively in North America and added the name of each place he visited to a large map on his studio wall. These travels provided the research material for the many books he illustrated. Whether he drew for *Canoe Country* (1938), or *As Far as the Yukon* (1951), written by his wife Florence Page Jaques, or for *John Burroughs' America* (1951), or for *John and William Bartram's America* (1957), he had a way of communicating the peace and beauty of the outdoors that he understood so well. He could also express himself in a small drawing. Look at Martin Bovey's *Whistling Wings* (1947). Here, Jaques captured the delight of duck and goose hunting in a series of stark vignettes. A single scene shows the thrill of the flock of blue geese "dropping toward us on stiffened wings . . ." to look over the Indians' decoy.

ROBIN JACQUES   *Vanity Fair*, line drawings, 5¾ × 8¾ inches, 1963

A superb draftsman and cartographer, Robin Jacques is completely at home in the nineteenth century and takes great pains to bring Thackeray's world alive for us. He is always lavish with clothes, accessories, and architectural façades. His characters wear stylish silk gowns, ostrich-plummed bonnets, crepe-bound hats, and dandified suits and uniforms. They live and have their little intrigues in mansions filled with bibelots and carved, polished furniture, and ornate paneling and wainscoting.

In these settings, with his flair for caricature, Robin Jacques does a variety of scenes of high life, love-making, comedy, and squabbles, to illuminate the scope of *Vanity Fair*. Pictured here, the astonished and imperious Miss Crawley asks Sir Pitt to kneel once more in a proposal to Becky Sharp. Sir Pitt explains the situation good humoredly while Becky hides behind him in humility and Miss Briggs continues eavesdropping.

When this artist works with color, as in Kipling's *Kim* and Turgenev's *Torrents of Spring*, he paints with the most delicate tints of watercolor.

FRITZ KREDEL *The Singular Adventures of Baron Munchausen,*
line in color separation, 6⅜ × 9⅝ inches, 1952

Fritz Kredel enters into the spirit of these adventures with exuberance. He matches in drawing
any exaggeration or exploit of Baron Munchausen, the man of fabulous action.

   The first episode takes place in the Russian countryside. The night before, snow had fallen
heavily. The baron had tied his horse to what he thought was a tree stump. By morning the snow
has melted. The baron finds his horse tied to a church steeple, uncomfortably straddling the cupola.

   Every detail of the story is there. The Russians, in greatcoats and fur hats, are highly amused
while the baron in regimental uniform shoots off the halter to bring down his horse.

   For the Limited Editions Club, Kredel has exquisitely colored this scene with a full palette.
In the reproduction above for the Heritage Press, he proves a master of color separation. Artists
are often tempted to apply second and third colors copiously. Not Kredel. He dips his brush
sparingly into pots of chocolate brown and beige and frames the white areas in black line to create
an illusion of snow in the churchyard, on the wall, and in thick patches on the roof.

IF ANYTHING, the wind and sea increased that night. Motionless in the narrow cockpit, drenched by the flying spray of icy seas, chilled by the wind, four hours seemed eternity. A liner passed us to the westward bound for Sydney, a slowly pitching carnival of light; passed and was lost again over the black rim of the world. How dark it is!

A low light is burning in the cabin; and in the binnacle a feeble lamp. Squalls strike us; the lamp flickers and goes almost out. There are no stars. You watch the compass card; and all the rest of the universe is sound and feeling. Feeling of wind and wet and cold, feeling of lifting seas and steep descents, of rolling over as the wind gusts hit; and sound?—of wind in the shrouds, of hard spray flung on drum-tight canvas, of rushing water at the scuppers, of the gale shearing a tormented sea.

✻ 26 ✻

ROCKWELL KENT *N by E,*
line drawings and woodcuts,
6 × 8¼ inches, 1930

That a book of adventure be splendidly written
and profusely illustrated with inspiration and
imagination by one and the same man is a rare
achievement. Rockwell Kent tells the story of
his "actual voyage to Greenland in a small boat"
and, to supplement the telling, heads each
chapter with a drawing of such feeling and detail
that the reader travels with him. He suffers
angry seas, masters navigation, charts, and
sextants, experiences the lifting of the fog, and
feasts his eyes on the serene landscapes of
Labrador and Greenland. As on any voyage,
there are leisurely moments for the meeting of
characters, for reminiscences and asides, and for
the companionship of the gentle Eskimo people.
Magically Rockwell Kent communicates the
inner peace that comes over man in the presence
of profound beauty and in communion with
the universe.

All this he conveys in line that is black and
fierce or light and graceful. He uses sharp lines
to catch the shimmer of sunshine over the
horizon or to depict the rolling sea, as in the
scene here with the skipper fighting the squall.
He works in rounder, softer patterns for the
fiords and mountains of Greenland and the snug
houses there. In the scene to the right, he turns
to the woodcut for the supplementary and
symbolic with the sun breaking through the
clouds as man looks wondrously, in "Hail and
Farewell," on the glory of the land once more.

Equally masterly in comprehension and
design are his *Candide, Moby Dick, Canterbury
Tales,* and *Complete Works of William Shakespeare.* His work was out of fashion for a while.
Now he is appreciated again. One publisher
has reissued his *Voyaging;* another is considering
a new edition of his *Wilderness.*

HENRY KOERNER   *Tracy's Tiger*, line drawings, 5 × 7⅜ inches, 1951

When Saroyan's *Tracy's Tiger* was published in 1951, it was unusual to find illustrations in a first
edition of a novel (as indeed it is today). Henry Koerner's contribution lay in his ability to provide
the New York scene so necessary to the background of the novel. He is a painter who likes to
draw from life and works quickly and freely in line with the gusto and spontaneity that suit
Saroyan's story. He fills the drawings with people—honest, struggling, bewildered, and sad—
in day-to-day city living, and he has a way of working landmarks like St. Patrick's Cathedral and

Bellevue Hospital into the scene at eye level so that the characters are breathing and working right in their midst. Above all he is sympathetic to Saroyan's fantasy and handles the theme of love wistfully in the symbol of the tiger, first imaginary and then real.

Koerner can do almost transparent drawings where one object is over another with both clearly defined. At the store for animal paintings, the glass door is closed but through it we can see Tracy at last united with Laura and the tiger at their feet. The drawing of the ice-cream parlor chair in no way breaks up the line of the store front.

LYNTON LAMB   *Tono-Bungay*, line drawings and
line in color separation, 6¾ × 9¾ inches, 1960

As one reads this book, one is moved by every illustration. Gentle, impressionistic, the drawings and color plates illuminate the moment, define the characters, and present the modes and customs of England, from Victorian upper-class rituals to the life of the working people and the use of the aeroplane before 1909. The drawings, small, compact, and in a staccato line, are set cosily within the text and are complete scenes that show Lamb's keen observation.

The sixteen color plates for the Limited Editions Club give the illusion of paintings that only an expert in graphic reproduction could detect as line in color separation. Lynton Lamb, the painter, understands composition and is able to translate the "tone and mass" of a painting into color separation. Disciplined and interested in bookmaking, he prepares the art for each plate in four separate drawings so that as each piece prints, the three colors and black mix and blend as in painting. For a more varied palette, Lamb chooses a different set of colors for each group of four plates. Subtly the colors reflect the structure and themes of H. G. Wells's novel. Ice blue predominates for the Victorian period, with the great house, its balustrades, and entrance gates. As George Ponderevo and his uncle Edward struggle to succeed, the mood changes to peach and olive brown. In the plate shown here, George is with his bride. The tenderness of their new relationship is evident. In the background the hansom cab moves swiftly through the London street with the gas lamps aglow. For "The Great Days of Tono-Bungay" the palette includes luxurious Nile green and warm grey, and for "The Aftermath" a turquoise and a vivid green symbolic of George Ponderevo's acceptance of what had to end. By the time one closes the book, one has long been aware of Lamb's warmth and understanding of the story.

Lynton Lamb has illustrated many fine books and has written *Drawing for Illustration* and *Preparation for Painting*, both sensible and lucid guides for any illustrator.

DAVID LEVINE *Smetana and the Beetles,* line drawings, 6½ × 8⅛ inches, 1967

David Levine has a way of bringing to the twentieth century the nineteenth-century art of caricature. Like Thomas Nast (1840–1902), the American caricaturist, illustrator, and painter, Levine is a man of many talents. He contributes his satirical cartoons to current periodicals, he paints seriously, and he is a forceful illustrator. In *Smetana and the Beetles* each drawing, lovable and exaggerated, embellishes Albert Kahn's adult fairy tale. Uncluttered and bold, they are also a statement in their own right of illustrious people in today's world and would be an addition to any art collection.

CHARLES PICKARD
The Call of the Wild,
line drawings and line in
color separation, 5½ × 8¼ inches, 1968

Charles Pickard captures the dramatic
moment so necessary for a Jack London
adventure. In this savage fight to the
death the mighty Buck leaps at the
throat of Spitz, the leader of the dog
team. We read on intently for the
outcome.

The artist is fascinated with the
Klondike and has done his research
thoroughly. His line has vigor as he does
the roughest of sketches and then
concentrates on the finished drawings.
He uses realism to portray Buck's fury
and frenzy when driven courageously to
action. For the mood scenes he works in
line like an impressionist. The illustrations
resemble black and white paintings in
which we follow the dog team struggling
through the snow-covered Yukon or
watch Buck swimming the rapids to
save the master he worships.

For the color plates Pickard starts
with a realistic drawing to which he adds
color overlays in a poster technique.
He includes a noble, haunting portrait of
Buck, symbolic of the wild and tame
heritage of all dogs.

The artist has illustrated Jack London's
White Fang with equal involvement.

HENRY C. PITZ
The Chronicles of Froissart,
line drawings and charcoal and
wash in color separation,
7¼ × 11 inches, 1959

Henry Pitz's illustrations for Froissart's
Chronicles covering the first half of the
Hundred Years' War and including the
battles of Crécy and Agincourt—two of
the greatest in history—tell as much of a
story as the scenes in the Bayeux tapestry
do of the Norman invasion of England.
This book is a treasure to examine closely
and the illustrations are essential to the
history. Fifteen color tableaux include
the battles and skirmishes on land and at
sea and the "diversities of the countries"
Froissart saw in his initial travels.

Pitz uses the entire page to stage the
English assault on the Norman town of
Carentan and creates the illusion of
frenzied action in the heat of battle. The
armored knight seems almost life-size as
he commands his pikemen and archers
to besiege the castle.

The touches of color, vermilion and
turquoise, heighten the excitement and
furor. Pitz applies them judiciously to

the banners waving in the breeze and to the soldiers' tunics. He adds a flesh tone to heighten the faces and to give aura to the background. The *pouchoir* method, a French hand-coloring by stencil rarely used in America, makes the freshness of color possible. As Pitz is an expert in color separation, he knew how to prepare his key plate as a wash drawing with charcoal texture. The Limited Editions Club had the drawings printed by gravure to retain the delicate gradations of tone. Then, on a set of proofs, the artist hand-colored each scene. At the *pouchoir* studio, trained workers cut stencils for each of the five colors with some overlapping of color and brushed on the colors by hand for each tableau.

A devoted student of the American painter and book illustrator Howard Pyle and an admirer of N. C. Wyeth, Pitz brings to the "period" book especially, an enthusiasm that penetrates each painting and drawing. A painter, a teacher, and the author of *Ink Drawing Techniques* and *The Brandywine Tradition,* he continues to encourage and guide the young illustrator.

PHILIP REISMAN *Crime and Punishment*, pencil drawing, 4½ × 7½ inches, 1944

Muralist and illustrator, Philip Reisman considers "the art of story-telling in pictures" as important as painting. He acknowledges as his masters Giotto, Rembrandt, Goya, Daumier, Doré, and Howard Pyle. In their tradition he contributed to this great book forty-one vital episodes for the 1944 Illustrated Modern Library edition.

Enamoured with the realism of Dostoyevsky, he fills the small pages with vivid scenes in different tones of black accented in line. The characters emerge in their daily life of poverty, elegance, and distress, in the streets and furnished rooms of St. Petersburg, in encounters with other boarders, relatives, priests, pompous functionaries, and the dying. We see in detail the badly dressed young student Rodon Raskolnikov commit the two murders. We watch him inwardly tormented until he confesses his deeds and gradually works out his repentance. Withdrawn and preoccupied, at this dinner in memory of a lodger's recent death, Raskolnikov sits silent and oblivious to the ridiculous scene in which the other lodgers drink and feast like gluttons.

Text within the drawing:

THE WORDS OF THE PREACHER, THE SON OF DAVID, KING IN JERUSALEM

VANITY OF VANITIES SAITH THE PREACHER, ALL IS VANITY

THE SUN ALSO ARISETH AND THE SUN GOETH DOWN

ONE GENERATION PASSETH AWAY AND ANOTHER GENERATION COMETH

BRIAN ROBB   *Ecclesiastes*, wash drawings, 5¾ × 9¼ inches, 1968

Brian Robb, a painter who has from time to time illustrated books, works in wash with accents of line but with the richness and depth of a complete color palette. With great feeling he approaches Numbers, Esther and Ecclesiastes for *The Oxford Illustrated Old Testament*. What is so refreshing is his presentation of Ecclesiastes. In the tradition of the Old Masters he illustrates the impressive imagery, and, following the style of the medieval illuminated manuscripts, includes certain of the significant sayings in his hand-lettering.

For the opening chapter even the shape of the drawing suggests a commandment worked on stone. Each scene becomes a storytelling: here, as the setting sun will rise again on the morrow, so the elder generation gives way to stalwart youth and the cycle of life continues. That this book reflects the thoughts of a worldly man is obvious from the clothes, houses, abundance of food, vineyards, and livestock that Robb intricately and colorfully works into the scenes.

LEONARD ROSOMAN
Point Counter Point,
line drawings,
5½ × 8¾ inches, 1958

For Leonard Rosoman, an incident becomes a
whole story in a picture. In this scene of the
nineteen-twenties with its elegance of pearls,
bracelets, silken dresses, carefully finger-waved
hair, gilt picture frame and mantlepiece bouquet,
the real selves emerge from behind the party
masks. The charming Lucy Tantamount is
observing her uncle, the painter Sir John
Bidlake, with a monocle glittering in his eye as
he looks disdainfully at the massive Mrs. Better-
ton. This older lady is still the naïve, vapid girl
whom Sir John knew twenty-five years ago
when he painted the "Bathers" now hanging
above the mantelpiece and reminding him of his
diminishing powers. Rosoman does a number
of equally brilliant picture stories for this book
that are the essence of Huxley's cynicism.

Leonard Rosoman considers book illustration
a serious métier. "I think I regard myself as a
painter who is interested in illustration—I would
almost go to the length of saying that it is
necessary for an illustrator to be a painter."
Preparatory to drawing, Rosoman does two or
three readings of a manuscript and delves into
his large reference library to research it. It is
with deep feeling that he starts a composition,
always larger in size than the actual reproduction will be. He lists as his finest work the
English translation of Charles-Louis Philippe's
Bubu of Montparnasse. He was overjoyed to
make wash drawings for Exodus and Chronicles
in *The Oxford Illustrated Old Testament*. As a
child reading the Bible left a fearful impression
on him and he appreciated the opportunity
"that, for once, everything that I had to say
would go into a book."

CYRIL SATORSKY
Leviticus,
line drawings, 5¾ × 9¼ inches, 1968

Satorsky is explicit and impressive in his presentation of Leviticus for *The Oxford Illustrated Old Testament*. With stirring emotion he draws as if he were listening along with Moses to the Lord speaking from the Tabernacle of the congregation. The ritual for the Feast of the New Moon shall be forever indelible. "In the seventh month, in the first day of the month" there shall be a day of "blowing of trumpets."

Satorsky has a way of combining realism with decoration. He uses patterns and textures—the carvings on the shophar, the stylized curls of the beard, the puffs of sacrificial smoke, and the assemblage of priests—to emphasize the solemnity of the occasion. In other studies for Leviticus Satorsky delineates the position of the hands as "a mystical sign still made even to this day during curtain prayers," the ritual of animal sacrifice, and the various food prohibitions for people of the Jewish faith.

In Chronicles, as it appears in the second volume of *The Oxford Illustrated Old Testament*, the decorative style becomes dramatically symbolic as Satorsky glorifies the kingdoms of Israel and Judah.

JOHN SCHOENHERR
Rascal, line drawings,
5⅜ × 8 inches, 1963

John Schoenherr is that adventurous combination of artist by profession and naturalist by avocation. He has the experience and the sentiment to be captivated by this tale of a raccoon named Rascal and Sterling North as a young boy during World War I.

For these reminiscences he works in scratchboard, a technique that involves painting a large area in black on a board with a chalky finish and scratching away the lines that are to be white. The drawings, natural and appealing, have the air of nostalgia that we associate with looking through a family album.

A year before Schoenherr accepted the assignment to illustrate *Rascal*, he visited Sterling North's native Wisconsin and instinctively absorbed the milieu of the wild woodland settings. In November when he started drawing, raccoons were already in hibernation. He relied on his memory, made trips to the zoo, and kept outside his house a raccoon skin to study textures and markings. This rendering of Rascal is just the way a raccoon would sunbathe on a branch: his tail hangs straight behind and "all four legs dangle over the sides in easy balance."

For Robert Murphy's *The Golden Eagle* and for Daniel P. Mannix's *The Fox and the Hound* Schoenherr's style changes to dramatic, dazzling brush painting, and his jacket watercolors show the same innate understanding of wildlife.

SUSANNE SUBA
Morning Faces,
line drawings,
5⅜ × 8 inches, 1949

Susanne Suba views the particular
moment through the eyes of the author
and presents it with clarity in fluid line.
For John Mason Brown's *Morning Faces*
she recalls his many cherished memories
as in this drawing of the summer parting
from "Cassie 13." With a mere suggestion of detail she conveys the entire
episode—the "good" boat tied to the
sturdy, high dock, the little and proud
fishermen, the knowing adults. She
leaves a catch in our throats.

Her imagination touched with humor
has great range. She captures the begin-
nings of time in Gerald Heard's *Gabriel
and the Creatures* (1952), the elegance of a
bygone era in Emily Eden's *The Semi-
Attached Couple* (1947), and the charm
and pleasures of Helene MacClean's
guidebook, *There's No Place Like Paris*
(1951). Susanne Suba has illustrated more
than a hundred books, each distinguished
by her interpretation of its subject and
each showing her affection for the
making of a book.

*"Good-by, Cassie B. Have a
nice winter and be a good boat"*

RONALD SEARLE   *The Anger of Achilles*, line drawings, 6⅛ × 9¼ inches, 1959

The Anger of Achilles is a spirited book in which translator and artist are equal contributors. Who else but Searle could be satirical and poke fun with the same ingenuity as Robert Graves?

The poet considers Homer a professional storyteller and *The Iliad* a "tragedy salted with humor." Graves's translation in prose and verse is for pleasure and Searle accompanies it in drawings as witty and incisive as his line is sharp. He depicts sorrow, fear, humiliation, boredom, seduction, voluptuousness, confession, humor, warfare, punishment, torment, and murder. There are many engaging moments—Zeus raging while Hera watches in boredom; the Amazonian Athena driving the chariot to help Diomedes in battle.

The gods give mortals "divine inspiration and divine possession" and Searle portrays them as superhumans who sweep down from Mount Olympus to mix in the fray. He faithfully adheres to the text and teasingly exaggerates and parodies the tunics, swords, breastplates, helmets, and chariots of ancient Greece. For Book One, the Owl-Eyed Athene, to prevent the murder of Agamemnon, pulls Achilles by the hair as he attempts to draw his sword. Searle entwines the resplendent, ferocious-looking helmet and the solid sword and spear with florid decoration.

In the tradition of English humorists stemming from the eighteenth-century caricaturist, painter, and book illustrator Thomas Rowlandson, Searle works at his drawings with gusto. In his own books, *Which Way Did He Go?* and *It Must Be True*, one discovers how he delightfully adds to reality his vision of truth.

BOOK ONE

Athene intervenes in the quarrel between Achilles and Agamemnon.

WHAT IS A MUMRUFFIN?

A *mumruffin* is a long-tailed tit which often visits
bird tables in winter for its share of *pobbies*.

WHAT ARE POBBIES?

Pobbies are small pieces of bread *thrumbled* up with
milk and fed to birds and baby animals.

WHAT IS THRUMBLED?

Thrumbled is squashed together. Ants thrumble
round a piece of bread, and crowds
in streets thrumble round *gongoozlers*.

46

BEN SHAHN   *Ounce Dice Trice*, line drawings, 7½ × 10 inches, 1958

That Ben Shahn was a communicator in pictures is evident in his paintings, murals, serigraphs, lithographs, stained-glass windows, and book illustrations. The making of a book was something special to him and he put every effort into its conception and execution. Once he accepted a text, he took time to make an actual book and thereby could experience the relationship between illustration and type page.

   In the nineteenth century there was no process available to reduce drawings as there is today. When an artist made his own wood engravings and then used them for printing plates, he had to work actual size. Shahn found this a logical procedure and for this historic reason made the sketches actual size. Then Shahn copied the text in his own distinctive lettering and fastened the separate pages of drawings and lettering securely so that when he opened the crude but solid binding, there was a readable handmade book. Sometimes his lettering appeared in the printed version as in Louis Untermeyer's *Love Sonnets*.

A *gongoozler* is an idle person who
is always stopping in the street
and staring at a curious object
like a *tingle-airey*.

47

Here, the selection from *Ounce Dice Trice* is an example of his expressive, descriptive, and versatile line style. We see action at several levels; the mumruffin swings above, the hands make pobbies which the ants eat on the ground, while at our eye level a gongoozler stares at us.

Shahn was most appreciative of the reproductive process learned in the days when he was an apprentice in a lithographer's shop. When a publisher requested color separation, Shahn prepared the art so that the printed result was just what Shahn wanted.

Today we admire his many illustrated books since 1952 including Ish-Kishor's *A Boy of Old Prague* (1963), Shahn's own *Love and Joy about Letters* (1963), and *The Shape of Content* (1957). They look distinguished, effortless, and contemporary. Behind them is a devotion, continuity, and persistence, as seen in his celebrated *Haggadah*. More than thirty years ago he prepared eleven beautiful, translucent watercolors for *Haggadah* but, as no publisher could afford to reproduce it then, Shahn set it aside. In 1958 he mentioned the project to the Trianon Press and was able to complete the illustrations for publication in 1966.

MARC SIMONT
The Wonderful O,
wash drawings in
color separation,
5⅜ × 8¼ inches, 1957

For the artist the most elusive and taxing assignment is the adult fable. To make it come alive, he must blend reality and legend with spontaneity and magic. *The Wonderful O* is one of those rare books in which the artist and observer of folkways Marc Simont inhabits the imaginative world of James Thurber and helps make the fable a statement of our time.

He wields pen and brush separately and together in a style that moves with the pace of the story and reflects humor, mystery, anger, fear, teachery, destruction, joy, and incredibility. In this final scene and climax, done with the lightest of grey and blue washes, he pictures the tribute to freedom, the wonderful O, glowing in the sunset as the elderly man reminisces with the inquisitive children.

In 1965 Simont wrote his own book *Afternoon in Spain* and illustrated it with a bold hand.

"Was it a battle? And did we win?" the children cried.

The old man shook his head and sighed, "I'm not as young as I used to be, and the years gone by are a mystery, but 'twas a famous victory."

The sun went down, and its golden glow lighted with fire the wonderful O.

72

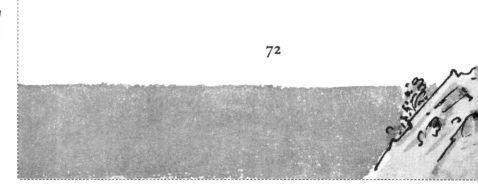

FELIKS TOPOLSKI
Pygmalion,
line drawings, 4¼ × 7⅛ inches, 1942

Bernard Shaw was one of the first patrons in
England of the Polish-born artist Feliks
Topolski. As a result there appeared this small
treasure of a *Pygmalion* for Penguin Books in
1942 with more than a hundred drawings in a
pictorial accompaniment as keen as the
dialogue. Nowhere is this more apparent than
in the famous scene where Colonel Pickering
escorts Eliza Doolittle to her supreme test.
We suddenly see Eliza as a ravishing Edwardian
lady who arrives at the embassy, meets the
fashionable, confronts first and second footmen,
and passes through the salons. Rightly for this
play, the illustrations become a procession of

PICKERING. Is this fellow really an expert? Can he ⬛
out Eliza and blackmail her?

HIGGINS. We shall see. If he finds her out I lose ⬛
bet.
Eliza comes from the cloakroom and joins them.

PYGMALION   95

PICKERING. Well, Eliza, now for it. Are you ready?

LIZA. Are you nervous, Colonel?

PICKERING. Frightfully. I feel exactly as I felt before my
t battle. It's the first time that frightens.

LIZA. It is not the first time for me, Colonel. I have done
s fifty times—hundreds of times—in my little piggery in
gel Court in my day-dreams. I am in a dream now.
omise me not to let Professor Higgins wake me; for if
does I shall forget everything and talk as I used to in
tury Lane.

PICKERING. Not a word, Higgins. [*To Eliza*] Now, ready?

LIZA. Ready.

PICKERING. Go.

They mount the stairs, Higgins last.
ckering whispers to the footman on the
st landing.

FIRST LANDING FOOTMAN. Miss Doo-
tle, Colonel Pickering, Professor
iggins.

SECOND LANDING FOOTMAN. Miss Doo-
ttle, Colonel Pickering, Professor
iggins.

At the top of the staircase the Ambassa-

people, a clue to the future direction of
Topolski's work.

Always able to catch the entire moment,
Topolski soon turned to pictorial journalism.
As early as 1953 he published his bimonthly
"Chronicles," four-page broadsides on the
political climate all over the world. In 1968 he
was responsible, along with the writer Conor
Cruise O'Brien, for the graphic and verbal
account, *The United Nations Sacred Drama*. His
frontispiece, done as a huge, circular painting to
symbolize the spectacle of the United Nations,
has the same palette of glowing crimson,
vermilion, and azure blue as he used in the vivid
coronation mural for Buckingham Palace in
1958. Similar and equally spectacular is *Holy
China* which he wrote and illustrated in 1968.

LYND WARD *Gods' Man*, woodcuts, 5½ × 8⅜ inches, 1966

If one wants to be a storyteller in pictures, what a great challenge it is to do it without text. In 1929 Lynd Ward did just that for *Gods' Man*, the first book of its kind in America, and later for two other novels. His woodcuts were used as the printing plates on a rich paper. These handsome editions are now collector's items. In 1966 and 1967 World reissued *Gods' Man* and *Wild Pilgrimage* in trade editions. Lynd Ward supplied prints from the original woodcuts for offset reproduction. The special quality of the woodcut printing on the paper has been modified but the novels are as alive and effective as social satires as if they had been drawn today.

In *Gods' Man*, except for five part titles, there is not one line of text. One hundred and thirty-nine woodcuts on right-hand pages tell the story. The woodcut can be a harsh medium with the delineation of faces and small details often crude and exaggerated. Lynd Ward turns this to advantage. Characterization emerges and each page, a complete study, always powerful and dramatic and at times spiritually beautiful, moves the story along until the final moment, portrayed here, when the young artist discovers the brand of the devil is within him and he must destroy himself. At the end the reader is emotionally spent with much to ponder about and with the desire to reread the storytelling pictures time and again.

LYND WARD *Gargantua & Pantagruel*, brush drawings, 6 × 9¼ inches, 1942

Lynd Ward works as effectively in the more conventional mediums of line, watercolor, and two-color drawings. For the Heritage Press edition of *Gargantua & Pantagruel* he chose a robust brush style to convey the satire of another era, with a sense of the grotesque, comic, and bawdy totally appropriate to Rabelais's five books. His Gargantua and Pantagruel are giants who fill the entire page while the other characters and scenery are drawn on a Lilliputian scale.

What could be more rollicking and ribald a caricature of monasticism than Lynd Ward's study of Friar John saving his abbey from attack during the Picrochole war. The enemy have laid their standards aside and knocked out the heads of their drums to use as grape baskets. Friar John, "tall, slim, with a wide mouth and a great nose, bold, venturesome, deliberate . . . " goes forth "wielding the staff of the cross" with the might of a sledge hammer until singlehanded he destroys every soldier.

Lynd Ward, at ease with Herculean assignments, has also illustrated *Beowulf, Idylls of the King*, and a romantic and haunting *For Whom the Bell Tolls*.

THE *first* BOOK   81

and hacked away so lustily, they fell on all sides like so many nine-pins. Thwack to the right, thwack to the left, Friar John struck in the old-fashioned style of fencing; thwack, thwack, he felled them like so many hogs. He brained some, smashed the legs and arms of others,

broke a neck here, cracked a rib there. He flattened a nose or knocked an eye out, crushed a jaw or sent thirty-two teeth rattling down a bloody gullet. Some had their shoulderblades dislocated, others their thighs lammed to pulp, others their hips wrenched, others their arms battered beyond recognition. Let a wretched fellow seek hiding amid the densest vines and Friar John ripped him up the back, gutting him like a cur. Let another take to his heels and Friar John split his head

CAREL WEIGHT
Joshua,
line and wash drawings,
5¾ × 9¼ inches, 1968

The opening twenty-two pages of "The
Historical Books" in *The Oxford Illustrated Old Testament* are impressive in
their visual account of the Israelite
conquest of Canaan. For each of the first
eight chapters of Joshua, Carel Weight
does a pertinent drawing in a different
style. The book begins dramatically with
Joshua looking across the river Jordan
while the Lord gives him divine guidance.
There are other descriptive scenes:
Rahab befriending the messengers from
Israel in her house upon the wall of
Jericho; the miraculous parting of the
river Jordan as the Israelites cross it on
dry ground; finally, at the entrance to
the city of Ai, the casting down of the
king of Ai's body.

Most memorable is Weight's interpretation of the battle of Jericho. It is
believable that no wall could withstand
the din from a "long blast of the ram's
horn" by the seven priests, together with
the shouting of the people, and "the wall
fell down flat . . . ." In the artist's words,
"the illustrator, in addition, has to
choose the frozen significant moment in
time . . ." and Weight succeeds in doing
just that.

BRIAN WILDSMITH
Joshua, line drawings,
5¾ × 9¼ inches, 1968

In John Ryder's *Artists of a Certain Line*,
Wildsmith says of his work, "First of all
I find out as much as possible about the
subject to be tackled and then draw
mostly from memory."

Starting where artist Carel Weight
left off in Joshua for *The Oxford Illustrated Old Testament*, Wildsmith conveys
the essence of this terrifying history of
the Israelite invasion of Canaan. In his
portrayal of Joshua there is all the
grandeur of a king powerfully drawing
his bow. The pose and dress of Joshua
resemble those of the figures found on
ancient Assyrian and Babylonian gypsum
reliefs.

Brian Wildsmith stages realistic and
mighty battles, with warriors charging
on horseback or brandishing swords from
their chariots. As he depicts the division
of the land of Canaan, he turns to the
abstract. One looks down from above at
the fascinating pattern of allotment
within the cities and in the outlying
districts. Fittingly Wildsmith ends the
book with the elderly Joshua admonish-
ing the Israelites to "choose you this day
whom ye will serve" and their resolve
"we will serve the Lord."

JOSHUA 10

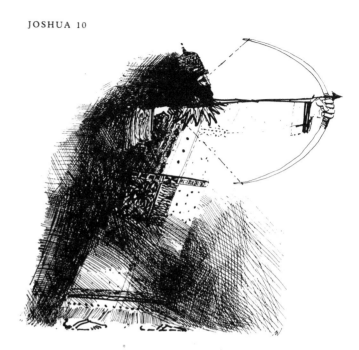

Jarmuth, the king of Lachish, and the king of Eglon. And it came
to pass, when they brought out those kings unto Joshua, that
Joshua called for all the men of Israel, and said unto the captains
of the men of war which went with him, "Come near, put your
feet upon the necks of these kings." And they came near, and put
their feet upon the necks of them. And Joshua said unto them,
"Fear not, nor be dismayed, be strong and of good courage: for
thus shall the LORD do to all your enemies against whom ye
fight." And afterward Joshua smote them, and slew them, and
hanged them on five trees: and they were hanging upon the trees
until the evening. And it came to pass at the time of the going down
of the sun, that Joshua commanded, and they took them down off
the trees, and cast them into the cave wherein they had been hid,
and laid great stones in the cave's mouth, which remain until
this very day.

And that day Joshua took Makkedah, and smote it with the edge
of the sword, and the king thereof he utterly destroyed, them, and
all the souls that were therein; he let none remain: and he did to
the king of Makkedah as he did unto the king of Jericho.

N. C. WYETH   *Trending into Maine*, line drawings and watercolor, 5¾ × 8⅝ inches, 1938

Every bit of knowledge, each experience and impression have bearing on an illustrator's work. N. C. Wyeth was a devotee of history and legend and a keen observer of life around him in the tradition of his teacher Howard Pyle. Kenneth Roberts' history, *Trending into Maine*, gave Wyeth the opportunity to express himself for the adult with the magic and romanticism we remember from his children's classics and to depict the Maine life he adored during summers spent at Port Clyde.

Always we are aware of the ever-changing seasons—glorious golden skies, waves softly breaking against the rocky coast, and snowy winters. In these settings with fresh, clear colors, Wyeth fills the historical paintings with action. For the contemporary studies he limits himself to one or two contemplative figures.

The somber scene of the lobsterman hauling in his traps does what storytelling illustration should do. In Kenneth Roberts' words, the land comes down to "a sea of pale blue satin and little wavelets run hesitatingly up the beaches." It is also a fine painting with light and shadow brilliantly manipulated—an earth-brown boat rocks on a teal blue sea fading to aquamarine. A morning mist enshrouds the foreboding pines, and the rocky coast recedes into an enchanted background.

EDWARD A. WILSON
A Journey to the Center of the Earth,
wash drawing with color separation,
6¾ × 10 inches, 1966

Edward A. Wilson slips into the nineteenth century for the eerie and realistic
touch to accompany the prosaic detail of
this science fiction. Each illustration is as
Jules Verne has described the scene and
each is romantically beautiful, unlike a
pop art or art nouveau approach that
would evoke horrific or weird associa-
tions. Here a luminous green tone over
the sepia painting creates a forest of
mystic darkness where the mushrooms
loom forty feet high and the men trudge
"in the intense cold shade." Only a
master of the book like Wilson can
control color separation to suit his needs.
By varying the color tones of his overlays from a glowing peach for the arrival
on a plain of lava to ice blue and cool
greys for the approach to the Icelandic
crater and the descent into the center of
the earth, the artist gives the illusion of
painting with a full-color palette. The
Heritage Press selected gravure printing
to obtain the full range of contrast
between the dark and light tones for the
sepia wash drawings and offset printing
for the large areas of flat color.

No matter whether Wilson works in
the bold woodcut style of *From Men and
Wooden Ships* (1924) or with watercolors
and a lithograph for *Treasure Island*
(1941), his representational art truly
enriches the text and reflects its spirit.

Supportive and Supplementary

JOSEPH ALBERS

JOHN ALCORN

EUGENE BERMAN

ANTONIO FRASCONI

ERIC GILL

MILTON GLASER

PAUL HOGARTH *(see also color section)*

EUGENE KARLIN

DONG KINGMAN *(see color section)*

CLARE LEIGHTON

LEONID

JOHN MINTON

JOSEPH LOW

JOHN PIPER

JUDITH SHAHN

WALTER STEIN

CHARLES WHITE

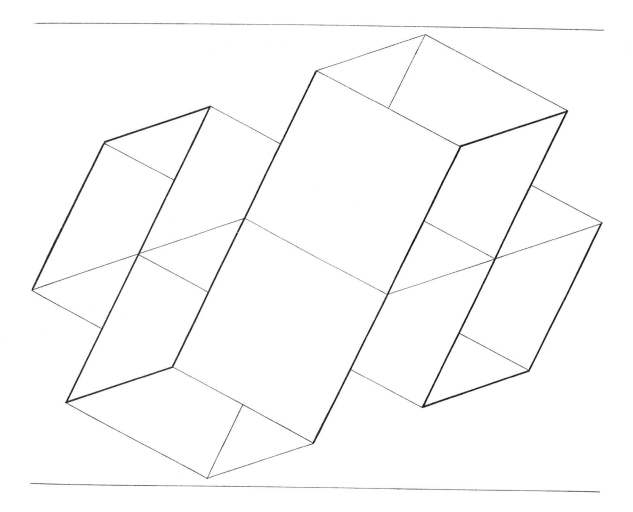

JOSEPH ALBERS   *Poems and Drawings*, line drawings, 9⅜ × 8⅛ inches, 1961

This visual treatment is imaginative and extremely personal. Albers, known for his series of paintings, "Homage to the Square," in which he stresses the interplay of colors, transfers this creativity into the interplay of line. He abstracts the feeling of motion expressed in some of his poetry.

In simple, concrete words, Albers poses deeper questions which he defines illustratively in the relationship of thick and thin lines. The poem

> One is walking
> one is standing
>
> who is more entitled
> to the path

accompanies this drawing. The lines appear to walk, to stand, and to walk again as one looks at them. For the other fourteen poems Albers meticulously constructs spatial variations, always enigmatical and fascinating.

JOHN ALCORN
The Abecedarian Book,
line drawings,
6½ × 8¼ inches, 1964

When John Alcorn designs and decorates a book, he takes responsibility for the entire *mise en pages* and deliberately creates an air of the turn of the century by borrowing from its advertisements and fashions. *The Abecedarian Book* by Charles W. Ferguson has style, a sense of order, and the ingredient of mischief that only Alcorn could concoct. The artist explains the meaning and derivation of the key words with his own graphic vocabulary of smiling suns, talking animals, and performing people. For the word "bioluminescent" he dips into a pot of realism and into a pot of fantasy to draw a whimsical explanation using a lightning bug "... giving off light from the very act of living." The intricate drawing and ruled borders in deep red complement the sedate black of the ornate initial and "period" type face of the facing page.

B is for **BIOLUMINESCENT**

The beauty of being a word detective is that if you keep your eyes and ears open, as every detective must, you can learn to use clues to find your way into and out of every big word. Clue is a word that can also be spelled clew, but however you spell it, it is the name for a ball of string. Once upon a time, in the tales the Greeks told about their gods, there was a mighty young warrior named Theseus who went into a deep cave with winding passages to slay a monster. Ariadne, a woman who loved him, gave Theseus a clue which he could unwind as he went along and then follow back to the entrance of the dark cave after he had slain the monster.

To find your way into and out of bioluminescent, begin with bio. The Greek word for life or living things was bios. Once you see bio in a word you know that the word has something to do with life or things that are alive. In biography, for example, bio combines with the Greek word graph, meaning write, and you have the written story of a man's life. Biology is a study of living things.

[7]

ERIK BLEGVAD   *The* Margaret Rudkin *Pepperidge Farm Cookbook,*
line drawings and watercolors, 7 × 10 inches, 1963

This book is an admirable example of anecdotal cookbook illustration. Margaret
Rudkin writes introductions to each section of recipes and occasionally pauses to
comment or to reminisce. It is Erik Blegvad who draws and paints hundreds
of stories, histories, customs, and explanations in the ample outside margins of
each of the four hundred and twenty-five pages. Starting with the binding, he
paints an open door in trompe l'oeil and invites us to step inside Pepperidge Farm
where there are chairs for us to sit down, and where we can either pitch in and
help with the preparations or eat a good meal. In realistic line or in bright watercolor vignettes he focuses on an object, a close-up of a scene or incident. We
watch children mischievously licking jam pots or helping to peel apples and
families merrily sharing meals and picnics. We examine complicated, simple,
and often antique utensils. Above all we are tempted by the luscious, colorful
ingredients—ripe strawberries, bouquets of cauliflowers, glistening eggplants,
freshly baked bread, wedges of cheddar cheese, well-hung meats, perky fowl,
and lively lobsters.

   Danish born Erik Blegvad, a frequent traveler on the Continent where he has
visited houses and their kitchens and, until recently, a Connecticut neighbor of
Mrs. Rudkin, is familiar with the milieu of her cookbook. For the part title,
"Country Life," he has delved into rural custom and imagined an old-fashioned
kitchen table and catch-all storage shelf that Mrs. Rudkin might have used in
1926. The liberties he takes and his idiosyncrasies make his work irresistible. He
adores cats and lets them wander about any scene regardless of the author's text.
Here they add warmth to the homelike atmosphere of mason jars, mixing bowls,
and sieve casually assembled and the fly avoiding the Flit gun.

PART TWO

COUNTRY LIFE

EDWARD BAWDEN

Gulliver's Travels,
lithographs in color separation,
5⅝ × 8¾ inches, 1965

Edward Bawden brings humor and a
personal involvement to each assignment. No matter how remote the era
or fanciful the tale, they come to life in
a panorama of activities. In the second
chapter of *Gulliver's Travels* the drawing
for the first voyage is like watching a
theatrical performance. The reader is in
Lilliput. Gulliver is confronted by the
Emperor, who boldly surveys him
beyond the length of chains while his
rearing horse is lead away, the
resplendent ladies and courtiers con-
verse, and the soldiers stand guard.
There is the quality of the fairy tale
here whereas in the voyages to the flying
island Laputa and the country of the
Houyhnhnms there are ample touches of
satire.

For the Folio Society's first edition of
Gulliver's Travels, Edward Bawden
drew the illustrations for just two of the
voyages directly on the litho plates. This
method provides the finest results because the artist makes his very own
printing plates for each color. These
original plates were later lost and
Bawden had the difficult task of imitat-
ing his own art by a different method
after a considerable lapse of time. Many
artists could not do this. Bawden re-
drew in color separation on plastocowell, a transparent plastic with a surface
similar to a lithographic plate used in
England, for offset reproduction. A man
of integrity, he feels the drawings for
the last two voyages are freer and more
spirited. For the reader the present book
is one of unity and glowing color with
pink, red, orange, yellow-gold, and blue
separate and overprinting on the black
key drawing.

ROBERT VERITY CLEM *The Shorebirds of North America*,
pencil drawings and watercolors, 9⅞ × 13⅞ inches, 1967

The editor and sponsor of this book, Gardner D. Stout, who had known and
admired Robert Verity Clem's work for many years, thought it fitting that the
artist should "illuminate a book devoted to shorebirds." For four years they traveled together around the United States while Clem observed the various species.

Spellbinding, these realistic paintings are extremely helpful in the study of
shorebirds. The birds, painted in opaque watercolor, look alive in their native
surroundings. Certain plates display two or more species that are seen together
on the sand and in the marshes. Others are devoted to one bird alone, like this
magnificent Upland Sandpiper on Plate XIV, who perches on a post where the
visibility is excellent to survey the quiet pastures of its territory. Sunlight dances
on the rock and the post; the barbed wire glistens and wildflowers bloom in
the tall grasses.

The design of the guide book is well thought out for the reader. The
paintings are placed sideways so that they are as large as possible and the minute
detail can be clearly seen. The bird names and explanations appear in a cor-
responding sideways position on the facing page for easy reference. Viking
printed the paintings richly in six colors.

SALVADOR DALI   *Essays of Michel de Montaigne*, line and watercolor, 6½ × 9½ inches, 1947

This is an unusual combination, a book of essays by a man of reason, selected and illustrated by an inner-directed surrealist painter and fabulous craftsman. It is a rewarding experience because Dali can express abstract ideas pictorially in a style that combines naturalism with illusion. He senses the self-exploration in Montaigne, which is that of all mankind. What could be more dramatic than this painting of the "conscience of a man" for the essay "On Repentance"? Here man in contemplation equates himself with the universe while a red man in the moon, a folk symbol, looks on.

Rightly the frontispiece suggests the depth and scope of the book. Dali superimposes a realistic portrait of Montaigne as Mayor of Bordeaux against his château and in contrast adds the bitter thrust of the title page drawing—a skeleton, the memento mori, seated on a turtle and with a live hand using a quill to write.

Equally penetrating are the other illustrations, always explosive, with an endless flow of piercing impressions, and executed with quickness and ease. The azure blue, vermilion, and flame interspersed with touches of shell pink and spring green—the colors of his palette—and Dali's grasp of composition stem from the Quattrocento.

Whenever and whatever Dali contributes to a book, it is with a fiery intensity and a keen sense of *mise en pages*, especially evident in the nineteen-forties, when he completed *Macbeth*, *The Autobiography of Benvenuto Cellini*, and Maurice Sandoz's *On the Verge*.

PAUL HOGARTH *A Russian Journey: From Suzdal to Samarkand,*
pencil and wash drawings and watercolors, 7¾ × 10⅛ inches, 1969

In the spring of 1967 author Alaric Jacob and artist Paul Hogarth traveled together across Russia. The outcome was *A Russian Journey*. Paul Hogarth relished working alongside the author and combining Alaric Jacob's word-picture with his own visual picture of a little known land, its people and architecture. The artist, sketching on location and adding finishing touches in hotel rooms, had every intention of drawing in black and white only. The Russian scene so fascinated him that he recorded it in watercolor too.

One hundred and fifty miles east of Moscow in Suzdal, Hogarth discovered the Spas-Efimovsky monastery, ". . . this vast troubled fortress built by Catherine II and used by the Tzars to bring incorrigible intellectuals to heel. So I saw it as an image which expressed my own personal feelings about imprisonment best . . . the actual watercolor was made rapidly with a pointed Japanese brush, using diluted and undiluted blotted washes of color, heightened with Faber Design Markettes. The great flocks of ravens and crows were drawn with a fully-charged brush of Higgins Eternal Ink and blotted; those in the far distance were drawn with a crow quill pen. I used Basingwerk Antique watercolor paper." Silhouetted against the white background stand the vividly colored rose-brick walls of the monastery with their sinister and brooding watch-towers and "central gateway sixty feet high."

Largely as a result of the drawing on this Russian trip, Hogarth felt the need to explain his experiences to fellow artists and wrote the explicit *Creative Pencil Drawing*

E. MCKNIGHT KAUFFER
Elsie and the Child,
drawings in stenciled color,
7½ × 10 inches, 1929

The American-born E. McKnight
Kauffer, trained as a painter in France
and Germany, went to England and
turned his talents to the poster. There
from 1926 to 1931 he illustrated five
books for the Nonesuch Press in which
he brought the stencil technique to
perfection. One of McKnight Kauffer's
most successful books was Arnold
Bennett's *Elsie and the Child* where he
purposely omitted a black key plate and
used black occasionally as one of the
colors. The stenciled illustrations are like
paintings in luscious silk screen colors
where shadow and light are created by
stippling. The frontispiece for *Elsie and
the Child* is not just a pretty picture but
an expression in McKnight Kauffer's
idiom of what the story is about. The
destiny of the characters will revolve
around this substantial Clerkenwell
home where there are two worlds: one,
that of the masters with their lace-
curtained drawing room and fine stone
steps leading to a formidable front door;
the other, the world of the servants confined to the basement by a spiked iron
railing.

When McKnight Kauffer returned to
America he worked in gouache for an
edition of W. H. Hudson's *Green
Mansions* and in watercolor for *Complete Poems and Stories of Edgar Allan
Poe*. Each of his books is different and
the illustrations are fitting to their subject. They are just as alive and powerful
today as when they were first drawn and
should be an inspiration to all book
illustrators.

ROBERT OSBORN   *Osborn on Leisure*, line drawings, photographs, watercolors,
10⅝ × 8 inches, 1956

Robert Osborn refers to himself as a drawer. When he creates his own books, his drawings project what a writer would say in words.

For *Osborn on Leisure* he defines leisure as a means "to further and enrich man's response to his own times and his own environment." In his drawings, watercolors, and occasional use of Old Master paintings, he explores, analyzes, and satirizes what is wrong with mankind today. He prods us into recognizing our errors and suggests solutions. His succinct text reinforces his picture stories. Instantly we identify with his characters, laugh at ourselves, and learn how much we lose by not taking time for leisure. We share his enthusiasms, his anguish, and his joy. How can we ever forget "the POWER of spring" as pictured here? There is no concern except that of surf casting in the quiet of the morning when the mist rises against the fresh, cool, stillness of the woods. The palette of greens is idyllic and tender in contrast to his vigorous line.

Robert Osborn makes adult picture books. A scholar and a serious painter, he turned humorist in 1941 when he illustrated and wrote how-to books on shooting and fishing. During World War II, he completed two thousand Navy posters and twenty-five training manuals containing the characters, Dilbert the Pilot and Spoiler the Mechanic. His first serious book was *War Is No Damn Good* (1946), then *Low and Inside* (1956), *The Vulgarians* (1960), and *Mankind May Never Make It* (1968). As in Daumier's lithographs and Goya's series of aquatints, "The Disasters of War," Osborn too gives each book a distinctive dramatic pace. Because of his gift, his ability to hit the mark, book publishers have asked him to illustrate many timely books including A. C. Spectorsky's *The Exurbanites* (1955) and John Keats's *The Insolent Chariots* (1958).

DONG KINGMAN *San Francisco: City on Golden Hills*, line drawings, wash drawings and watercolors, 8⅞ × 12¼ inches, 1967

There are times when a book is like a visit to an art gallery. *San Francisco* by Herb Caen is such an experience. Here the reader has the chance to view a considerable number of watercolors, wash drawings, and line sketches by Dong Kingman on his favorite subject, the golden city. A realist who has a sense of design that borders on abstraction, he conveys a lively enchantment with whimsy as he looks about the city. He paints majestic panoramas of the bay and the San Francisco hills. He captures the vertical structure of recent building, cherished landmarks, and close-ups of street scenes as if one were there on foot. Often he does the same site from a different angle. Utility wires dance in the breeze, kites fly over business districts, and flags flutter in the wind.

Dong Kingman has absolute control of his brush. Whether he paints in water-color or in black wash, the picture sparkles. The skies are clear, the bay is bright blue, the streets shimmer in sunshine and shadow, the traffic lights blink red and green. Along California Street the ornate reds and oranges of the Chinese pagoda-type buildings guide one down the vast hill past Grace Cathedral and to cross Grant Avenue to the everywhere present bay. Chortling, Dong King-man sees people dwarfed by the vastness of the landscape as they wend their way by foot or in car and trolley in and out of the blue-grey shadows.

Herb Caen rightly refers to Dong Kingman as a collaborator. The artist's view is a separate and equal contribution drawn especially for this informal look at present-day San Francisco, that includes previous paintings done as early as 1938 and 1946 to reveal his nostalgia and the changes that have taken place.

EUGENE BERMAN   *Rome and a Villa*, line drawings, 5⅜ × 7⅞ inches, 1952

Eugene Berman graces Eleanor Clark's *Rome and a Villa* to perfection with ten beautiful drawings. A neo-romanticist, he makes no attempt to portray the contemporary. Of greater importance, he depicts in an effortless line the essence of the past, the ancient ruins and grandeur of the High Renaissance and Baroque as they still exist today. With a knowledge of Rome equal to the author's, an affection that borders on worship for the city, and an understanding of the elements that make up its architecture, he captures the wholeness of a building with its intricate stonework as if we were there gazing at it. He sketches playing fountains with their water nymphs and tritons, obelisks and statuary, the sweep of a palazzo, and the elegiac cypresses that parallel the wall to Hadrian's villa.

A master of proportion and form, spontaneous, and demanding complete freedom of expression, Berman illustrates books including his own *Viaggio in Italia* (1951) and *Imaginary Promenades in Italy* (1957) with the same intensity that he paints or creates stage designs for theatre, opera, and ballet.

ANTONIO FRASCONI
Bestiary/Bestiario,
woodcuts in color separation,
8¼ × 11⅜ inches, 1965

When Frasconi illustrates a
book with woodcuts, one
reads it both visually and
verbally. Each page of the
Bestiary/Bestiario by Pablo
Neruda is a joy to behold; it
sparkles with intense black
and flaming red as if the artist
has just proved the woodcuts
in his studio and the ink still
glistens. Dedicated to the
actual making of a single
book by hand, he is appreciative of the help of Joe Blumenthal, the master of The Spiral
Press, who printed *Bestiary/
Bestiario* by letterpress and
achieved better results than if
Frasconi had hand-printed it.
    Frasconi visualizes his
themes with simplicity and
directness. His use of white
space is dramatic, his execu-

When I had feet for walking
in triple nights now past,
I followed the nocturnal dogs,
those squalid travelers
that trot in silence
with great haste traveling nowhere,
and I followed them for many hours.
They mistrusted me,
ah, poor stupid dogs,
they lost their opportunity
to pour out their sorrows,
to run through streets of ghosts
with grief and tail.

Cuando tuve pies para andar
en noches triples, ya pasadas,
seguí a los perros nocturnos,
esos escuálidos viajeros
que trotan viajando en silencio
con gran prisa a ninguna parte
y los seguí por muchas horas,
ellos desconfiaban de mí,
ay, pobres perros insensatos,
perdieron la oportunidad
de narrar sus melancolías,
de correr con pena y con cola
por las calles de los fantasmas.

tion is uncluttered, and his integration of woodcut with text makes each page a distinct addition to the book. As Neruda ponders the meaning of the universe, Frasconi accompanys the questions with concrete images. Flighty rabbits gambol through imaginary fields, a spider spins her starlike web, the frogs serenade, the birds express the joy of daybreak, and a nocturnal dog bays mournfully to the man in the moon.

He has given himself unsparingly to the book. Outstanding are his woodcuts for *12 Fables of Aesop* (1954), newly narrated by Glenway Westcott, and for his own *A Book of Many Suns* (1953), *Birds from My Homeland* (1958), *A Whitman Portrait* (1960), and *The Face of Edgar Allan Poe* (1960).

ERIC GILL   *The Four Gospels of the Lord Jesus Christ,*
line drawings, 9⅛ × 13⅛ inches, 1931

It was natural that Eric Gill should become concerned with the art of the book.
Trained as an architect and skilled as a wood engraver and stone carver, he
believed the artist should also be a craftsman, able to execute the finished designs
in stone or wood. Gill enthusiastically did just that. A student of the English
calligrapher Edward Johnston, Gill designed several type faces including Gill
Sans Serif, Golden Cockerel, Perpetua, Johanna, and Bunyan which he specified
for the books he wrote, illustrated, and produced, and which are favored today by
many book designers. It was always a joy for him to plan, decorate, and draw
for the book, making it a pleasure to behold, peruse as well as read. Combining
the arts of decoration and illustration he brought gaiety and humor to *The
Canterbury Tales* and put his personal imprint on each pocket volume of Dent's
New Temple Shakespeare.

Deeply religious, he interpreted religious subjects with intensity. The book,
The Four Gospels, is a masterpiece. He makes the text an integral and graceful
part of the drawings by entwining around the verses scenes that are powerful and
vivid. For the gospel of Mark, using the heaviest blacks and the sharpest lines, he
composes the drawing around the initial A which rests upon the verse and
supports the ladder. Here is the drama of the crucifixion when the "many other
women" and Joseph of Arimathaea remove Jesus from the cross. The
mournful facial expressions, the flowing hair, the soft folds of the garments,
and the texture of the cross contrast with the well-proportioned letter forms
he designed. The impression is that of an illuminated manuscript.

NOW WHEN THE EVEN WAS COME

Fierce and Gentle Warriors,
wash drawings,
6⅛ × 9¼ inches, 1967

When Milton Glaser illustrates books, he prefers to set the mood rather than picture specific incidents in detail. For *Fierce and Gentle Warriors,* three stories by Mikhail Sholokhov, Glaser imparts a dimension of freedom and size to his paintings rarely found in a book. Sweeping across two pages for each study and using white space as if it were a second color, he paints eight somber and romantic impressions of the Cossacks, their life on the steppes, and the river Don that flows through their land. Typical of Russia there is the vastness and loneliness, the tenderness and gentleness, the sorrow and suffering. His illustrations make the reader curious. In the first story "The Colt," why are Trofim with his mare and colt in a jog trot and separated from the squadron of Cossacks brandishing their sabers in battle? What is this spirited colt doing in a war?

In a different vein, with a talent both decorative and flamboyant, Milton Glaser has embellished the theme of the ancient carol for *The Twelve Days of Christmas Cookbook.* Sporadically he has also edited and published a broadside, "The Push Pin Graphic," in which he has displayed his graphics and those of his colleagues at The Push Pin Studio.

PAUL HOGARTH *Majorca Observed*, line,
pencil and wash drawings, 6⅝ × 9½ inches, 1965

Paul Hogarth, who refers to himself as an artist-reporter, has a way of expressing himself in drawing so that the reader shares his visual experience. He accompanies Robert Graves in *Majorca Observed* with a lyric touch. He draws the unspoiled, tranquil island before World War II with its polite people in remote towns connected by narrow, winding roads, its orchards of almond, olive, and fig trees, and its windmills turning in the countryside. After the war, Hogarth notes the changes—the restless hoards of tourists, the enormous hotels, the utility wires marring the landscape, and the graphics of street signs and advertisements. Drawing spontaneously in pencil and in black ink or wash for emphasis, Hogarth gives the illusion of sketching quickly at the scene. This is not always so. Hogarth has taken as long as three hours to do a single drawing of a house so minute is the detail of decoration and material.

Selective, Hogarth includes only what is essential to make his point. Pictured here is the leisurely Plaza España in Palma with its ornate barometer as the focal point in the garden-like shade of the palm trees. In contrast, at the outermost edge are the automobiles and a mule-drawn cart. The intimacy and humor come from the details—the blades of grass, the lettering on the barometer and gateway, a lady's pocketbook.

Hogarth has traveled the world on assignments for *Life*, *Fortune*, and other publications. His understanding of people, custom, and terrain is so astute that even if he has not been to a country, he can research, interpret, and comment on it as he did in James Atwater's and Ramon Ruiz's book about Mexico, *Out from Under*. With *Brendan Behan's Island* and *Brendan Behan's New York* Hogarth is like a companion on the author's jaunts and gives richly of his intimate knowledge of the subjects. A painter and a teacher, he has written *Creative Ink Drawings*, a book as fascinating for its art as for its lucid and rewarding technical explanations.

EUGENE KARLIN
The Rubaiyat of Omar Khayyam,
line drawings,
6½ × 9 inches, 1964

Seemingly Eugene Karlin dips his pen
into the ink once and draws without
pause until he has finished an illustration.
From his pen, in the finest line, flow
scenes that show a beauty, tenderness,
and sensuality appropriate to *The
Rubaiyat*.

Karlin's approach to this oft-illustrated
poem is a combination of decoration and
storytelling. Aware of the tradition of
the illuminated Persian manuscript, the
artist repeats arabesque patterns and
themes. In the study here, ornamental
flowers and leaves on stylized branches
create an exotic garden within an imaginary framework against the white space
of the page. Omar Khayyam and his
love, drawn with the softest curves, pose,
glance, and gesture as in a tableau. Her
luxuriant flowing hair and the folds in
his turban emphasize the curves of the
drawing. The illustration is an episode
taken from one of the quatrains.

For the jacket Karlin repeats a line
drawing and tints it with delicate pastel
watercolors in the same style he has used
for children's books.

An enthusiastic teacher of art and book
illustration in New York City, Karlin
has made a sensitive interpretation of
love and friendship for Plato's *Lysis,
The Symposium, Phaedrus* (Limited
Editions Club, 1968). The drawings in an
ethereal grey never overpower a study of
the text but enhance it.

CLARE LEIGHTON
The Time of Man,
wood engravings,
5¾ × 8⅝ inches, 1945

As the lines of an engraving are visible to the human eye, so are an artist's feelings. That the English-born Clare Leighton loved the beauty of this book and was at her happiest working on it is evident. She has caught the rhythm of the land and its people, the essence of this poetic tale. She has given it her supple skill of engraving, her knowledge of Kentucky based on a nine-year stay in the South, and her admiration for Elizabeth Madox Roberts as a novelist.

Her interpretation is supportive illustration at its finest. With a mere suggestion of movement Clare Leighton pictures the farm girl with her heifer traveling staunchly over hill and dale to an unknown destination. For the rich blacks of the wood engravings the publisher provided a specially made cream rag paper and proper printing so as to make this twentieth-anniversary edition of the novel a celebration.

LEONID   *The Oysters of Locmariaquer*, pencil drawings, 5⅜ × 8 inches, 1964

Interpreting a book with illustrations is a highly individual process. Some artists will do dozens of drawings like a running commentary. Leonid makes a complete statement with a jacket and three textual drawings. Sparse and evocative, they describe to perfection the ritual of breeding and cultivating the oyster in Brittany. Leonid, a landscape painter of the neo-romantic movement, draws as if he were using a palette of black and white. He does not illustrate the legend or scientific observation that Eleanor Clark blends into her story-history, *The Oysters of Locmariaquer*. Instead, he is concerned with the gentle coastline, the immense expanse of shore, and the passive, low-lying sky. Above, silhouetted against the sky and water, an entire family works side by side at low tide. They scrape and tie the tiles for oyster breeding in the mud with quiet dedication as has been the custom since 1860.

In a still life Leonid examines a handful of oysters with the "jagged crenellation of the shell" and the reader marvels at the "fit of the two valves." On the flat surface of the jacket he creates texture as if he were painting on canvas. Treating it as an essential part of the book and using the second color to capture lights and shadows to their best advantage, the artist produces a study of the barges with their cargo of tiles glowing white in the dawn against the olive-grey background. Solemnly and slowly the barges make their way to where the oysters will be set to breed.

JOHN MINTON
French Country Cooking,
line drawings,
5⅛ × 7¾ inches, 1951

Cookbook illustrations should have two objectives: one to instruct and encourage; the other to picture the rewards of its labors. John Minton did both as he romantically and seriously decorated Elizabeth David's *French Country Cooking*. He took the reader traveling through the provinces, for a peek in the kitchen, to shop for ingredients and to share meals on grand occasions. Often in the background of a drawing he added a window and from it a nostalgic view of a familiar country scene. For the chapter on "Fish," perhaps these Frenchmen with their bottle of wine are angling for the carp, eel, and tench needed to make "matelote of River Fish." In the foreground there are other fresh fish, a lobster with tail still striking, condiments, and fish salvers. Minton used vignettes to teach one how to stir a sauce and add the wine. With a style as down to earth as kitchen utensils, he conveyed the honesty and goodness of French cooking appreciated by the author.

One never forgets a book with John Minton illustrations because the artist had the rare gift of stepping inside the author's world. He never spared himself but worked untiringly. This is especially true in *Time Was Away* (1948) which Alan Ross wrote and John Minton illustrated as a "day-to-day journal" of their visit to Corsica. One follows their tour of the island, absorbed by the intensity of the detailed landscapes and by the studies of apathetic people and children, and one basks in the sun-drenched color plates expertly prepared in separation.

JOSEPH LOW   *Directions to Servants,*
wash drawings in color separation, 6⅛ × 9 inches, 1964

Joseph Low fills the pages of Jonathan Swift's *Directions to Servants* with the
sauciest of character studies. Insolent butlers, angry cooks, bored footmen, surly
coachmen, sly chambermaids, and arrogant waiting maids go about their
unpleasantness at a lively pace. One chortles at the artist's sense of mischief, a
splendid accompaniment to the author's wit. One senses Joseph Low's intimacy
with another era as if he had stepped back into the eighteenth century and
steeped himself in the study of its clothes, cooking utensils, dishes, furniture,
houses, towns, and seaports. As shown here, the sullen cook is pondering how to
apply Swift's directives. The drawing is strong and flamboyant in deep brown line.
Joseph Low brushes on a wash of yellow-brown to add depth, body, and texture.

What is refreshing is Joseph Low's conception and design of a book. Every
page is a visual surprise with no set pattern as to size or style of drawing. Forty-
five drawings showing activity in a variety of ways alternate with pages of text.
There are montages, scenes, full-length portraits, and close-ups. One can look
through the book time and again and discover new meanings in the interplay of
color. As a printer at his Eden Hill Press, Joseph Low has studied what happens
when two colors mix in line or wash as they print. In *Directions to Servants* he
combines with daring and expertise the light and deep tones of yellow-brown
with the line and wash of dark brown and obtains results that have the richness
and range of full color painting.

One has only to read his credo, "Notes on the Eden Hill Press" for the journal,
Printing & Graphic Arts, to realize Low's effort and persistence with the art of the
book. Preferring the linoleum block for his own publications at the Eden Hill
Press, he has interpreted and created a brilliant and sensitive *Aesop: A Portfolio of
Color Prints* (1963) and is at work on another portfolio: *Aesop: Selected Fables.*

JOHN PIPER *The Natural History of Selborne,*
wash drawings, 6⅛ × 9¾ inches, 1962

John Piper is painting for an eighteenth-century book in a twentieth-century manner. In the nineteen-twenties and -thirties he was primarily an abstract painter. He also designed for the stage. As he became interested in English country architecture and landscape, he began to blend the abstract and the representational in both painting and book illustration. He uses this style enchantingly to illustrate the poetry of the English countryside that Gilbert White made famous in *The Natural History of Selborne.*

Drawing with an ethereal line over a soft wash background, Piper uses the surface of the paper for highlights. When he needs a vibrant touch, he dashes on other highlights by brushing on strokes of white over the dark landscapes. Lyric and mercurial, his black and white studies show immense knowledge and observation of Selborne from the first moment of spring until the early snow of November. There is the sensation of the moisture in the woods, of the trees heavy with their glossy foliage, of the lanes, the fields, the paths, the roads, the stone and brick cottages, of the stately houses, just as Gilbert White described them, set in the magnificence of the Hampshire countryside.

His handling of scenes is effervescent. He draws a single study or a composition in two parts that includes a favorite vista and a companion piece. He varies these with a sequence of two or three impressions, as in this drawing of Selborne Church. The upper view shows the exquisiteness of the Gothic architecture and the simple beehives in the midst of the summer verdure. In the lower view Piper abstracts an impression of Selborne Church that is like a cherished memory.

John Piper believes in the good book illustration that occurs when an artist expresses himself freely without compromise or conformity. Practical, he delves into the problem of color reproduction and suggests that "by whatever method, the artist should ask for a lively parallel to his work, not an imitation of it, in color or in any other particular. He should ask, in fact, for the same kind of result he would get if he translated a work of his own into another medium." A glance at Piper's full-color paintings for the Faber & Faber edition of "The Traveller" by Walter de la Mare shows in reproduction a brilliant and visionary use of color.

JUDITH SHAHN *Men of the Revolution*, line in color separation, 5½ × 8¼ inches, 1970

Judith Shahn does a study in contrasts for *Men of the Revolution*, the biographies of Porfirio Diaz, Zapata, Pancho Villa, and Victoriano Huerta, by John Tebbel and Ramon Ruiz. Her portraits convey the character of the stern, pompous reactionary despot, the courageous revolutionary, the dashing bandit, and the visionaries who become competent leaders. Moved by the bitterness and drama in this revolutionary period of Mexican history, Judith Shahn is sensitive to human injustice and depicts the poverty, suffering, and despair alongside the beauty and primitiveness of the country. Having gone to college in Mexico and later having lived there, and having great enthusiasm for its lithographs and block prints, she reports in her decorative style each historical scene as if she had been there watching.

Pictured above are the ragged peasants turned soldiers and traveling with their women as an army under the hero-leader Zapata. One feels the rhythm of the marching in bare feet and boots and senses the individuality of the peasants by the tilt of their sombreros. Observe the patterns of decoration in the hand-woven embroidery, the cartridge belts, and the repetition of black in the hair, shawls, and fluttering skirts. Purposely the artist introduces harsh diagonals to stress reality in a romantic scene. Her stark black and white figures are silhouetted against a pale olive-grey background and the effect of her drawing is that of a printed woodcut. This study is the theme of the jacket painting done in bright, gouache colors. Fortunately it is printed on the binding of the library and school editions too.

There are many other fascinating scenes, each a reflective comment on the revolution and on the ensuant building of republican Mexico.

WALTER STEIN   *Natural Histories*, pencil drawings, 8½ × 11⅜ inches, 1966

Artists are drawn to a book like Jules Renard's *Natural Histories*. It calls forth
the fascination the animal world has for them and gives them an opportunity to
display their talents in a series of drawings. Toulouse-Lautrec, Bonnard, and
Walter Stein each designed and illustrated Renard's observations for three different *livres de peintre* published in 1899, 1905, and 1960, respectively. With a
new translation by Richard Howard and a commentary by Edgar Munhall, all
their drawings are now in one book so that reader and illustrator may study,
compare, and benefit from a wealth of interpretations.

Here our discussion centers on the contemporary artist and painter Walter
Stein who presents the animals within his range of experience. He uses as models
his pet cat and dog, insects from his collection of mounted specimens, and wild
and exotic animals and birds confined in city zoos. Sensitive, alive, and with
piercing, sad eyes, the creatures stand in front of us and seem well aware of our
presence, our movements and our silences. The portraits, silhouetted against the
white pages, are so strong and dominant that in our imagination we fill in the
details of the landscape.

From Renard's fragment of text, Stein selects the essential point for his
impression of a stag with "his antlers like a dwarf tree whose branches have been
stripped of leaves." We know the stag is listening and watching us and suddenly
will take to the woods.

When Stein prepared these pencil drawings for the limited edition, the book
was another size, 10½ × 8½ inches, and included both original lithographs from
the paper plates on which he had drawn and offset lithographs reproduced by
expert commercial printing. The drawings in the present book printed by offset
communicate successfully although they do not have the ephemeral quality or
the recognizable pencil texture that results from the grainy lithographic surface
on which he worked.

In 1967 Walter Stein illustrated, designed, and published *Elegy* by Chidiock
Tichborne. In this volume Stein shows an ability to draw the human figure
delicately in very few lines.

CHARLES WHITE   *Four Took Freedom*, line and wash drawings, 5½ × 8¼ inches, 1967

Charles White is a drawer of themes. One has only to look through *Images of Dignity*, a collection of his sensitive drawings, to see the recurring themes of love, beauty, and hope. When he illustrates *Four Took Freedom*, the biographies of Harriet Tubman, Frederick Douglass, Robert Smalls, and Blanche K. Bruce, by Philip Sterling and Rayford Logan, he does not draw specific storytelling incidents but expresses his total conception based on his personal philosophy and his many years of experience as an artist. In his own words, "I use Negro subject matter because Negroes are closest to me. But I am trying to express a universal feeling through them, a meaning for all men. . . ."

His drawings enrich and grace the text with eloquence, dignity, and emotion not often found in illustrated biographies. Mr. White, a competent painter, prefers to work in black and white

Harriet led over 300 slaves to freedom and never lost a passenger.

with a variety of mediums: charcoal and Wolff crayon, ink, and linocut. Thus, he is at ease with the restrictions of the book. For the drawing pictures here, he uses black line with the tonal values of painting. Basing his study on the biblical theme of Moses leading the Jews to the Promised Land, he depicts a Harriet Tubman spiritually and physically guiding the slaves in their passage to freedom. Their faces reflect struggle and perseverance. Dressed in robes symbolic of deliverance, the success of their flight is indicated by the movements of their bodies and the motif of the outstretched hand in the foreground.

Charles White contributes other scenes in line, pensive or active, and four realistic portraits in a combination of line and wash. All the drawings complement the book and would be an addition to any art collection.

Instructive

ROBERT VERITY CLEM *(see color section)*
NORMAN IVES
GEORGE GIUSTI
JOHN LANGLEY HOWARD
ANTHONY RAVIELLI
SUZAN NOGUCHI SWAIN
MARY SUZUKI
EARL THOLLANDER

NORMAN IVES *Eight Symbols*, line in color separation, 8¾ × 8⅛ inches, 1960

Symbols are the language of design. As symbols convey attitude and mood and reflect the artist's philosophy, they become instructive and decorative illustration. They can be simple and direct. They are always an intense, economical form of communication.

Norman Ives, sculptor, printmaker, publisher of portfolios, and book designer, expresses himself in symbols. In his own book *Eight Symbols*, he forms certain variations of symbols that are potential trademarks for the worlds of finance, industry, and architecture. Aware that these trademarks will appear on letterheads and other printed media, on buildings and trucks, and on a variety of materials including "glass, fabric, wood, concrete, metal, and paper," he treats them imaginatively. In his hands the simple letter H below becomes a dynamic and powerful symbol representing a chain of hotels. Norman Ives accomplishes this by choosing a square serif letter that looks like a building block and by designing it in three dimensions with an interplay of color between the grey and black areas so that there is both an "illusion of double reading" and of action.

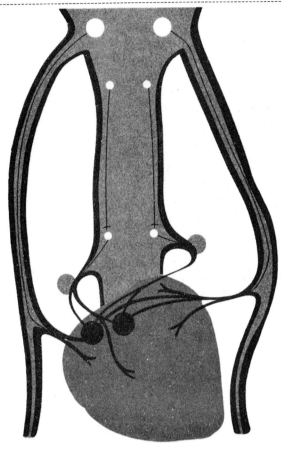

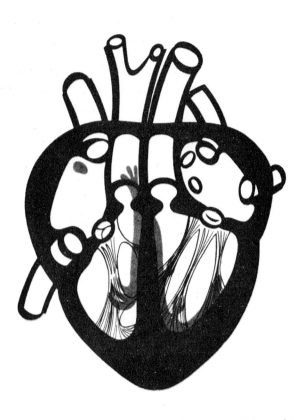

The rhythmic beating of the heart is initiated within the heart itself by some mechanism that is still unknown. The rate of beating, however, is controlled by nerves and by chemical substances within the blood. Two sets of nerves normally control the rate: one to speed it up, the other to slow it down. These nerves act on a special tissue in the right auricle that sets the pace of the heart by transmitting trigger impulses to the heart muscle.

Waves of impulses pass to the muscles of the auricles and to a second patch of tissue located in the partition between the right and left heart, which relays the impulses to the ventricular muscle. If these impulses are blocked by disease, the heart continues to beat slowly, but auricles and ventricles beat independently and lose their coordinated rhythm (cardiac arrhythmias).

GEORGE GIUSTI *Heart*, line in color separation and watercolor 4⅛ × 6½ inches, 1962

In 1962 Frederic Ditis coordinated illustration and written word with an artistic consultant for an international series of visual paperback books. A different artist worked with a leading authority on each of the factual studies, *Space*, *Anxiety*, *Genetics*, and *Heart*. The artist was free to plan his own *mise en pages* and to paint or draw as he wished.

Each volume is unique. *Heart* by George Giusti and Rudolf Hoffman, M.D., is the most dramatic. In it Giusti visualizes in design and illustration what medical history knows about the heart, its structure, function, and diseases. His diagrammatic drawings of people and their anatomy help one to "read" the pictures with the text. The basic outline of the heart is always in heavy black line; veins, arteries, and valves are shown in medium line; the ventricular muscles in thin line. Giusti applies color to heighten and emphasize the heart's functions and problems. He prefers a flamboyant palette of vermilion, blue-violet, magenta and violet. He illustrates this book with the brilliant and painstaking perception he has become famous for in poster design, institutional advertising, and book jackets.

JOHN LANGLEY HOWARD   *The Origins of Angling*,
watercolor, 8¼ × 10⅞ inches, 1957

Illustration for reference texts requires exacting and interpretive research by the
artist–illustrator. In preparation for these exquisitely realistic paintings of the
twelve modern trout flies, the authors used a method fascinating to scholars and
artists as well as anglers. A description of these trout flies had appeared in 1496
in the first printed version of *The Treatise of Fishing with an Angle*, attributed to
the fifteenth-century nun, Dame Juliana Berniers. In 1963 when John McDonald
wrote *The Origins of Angling* he asked Dwight Webster, a professor of fishery
biology, to analyze Dame Bernier's descriptions of trout flies. Heeding her
words ". . . dub them just as you will now hear me tell," Professor Webster tied
the flies with alternatives for John Langley Howard to paint. The flies appear
twice their size in the book so that the texture of the wings and body and the
natural and dyed colors of the wool can be compared with Dame Bernier's
instructions.

THE BERNERS TROUT FLIES

Tied by Dwight A. Webster—Painted by John Langley Howard

DUN FLY (March)

First Choice

Alternative One

Alternative Two

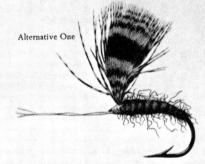
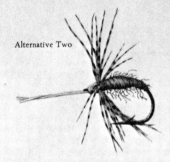

The donne flye the body of the donne woll & the wyngis of the pertryche

ANOTHER DUN FLY (March)

THE STONE FLY
(April)

A nother doone flye. the body of blacke
woll: the wynges of the blackyst drake: and
the Jay und the wynge & under the tayle.

The stone flye. the body of blacke wull:
& yelowe under the wynge. and under
the tayle & the wynges of the drake.

RUDDY FLY (May)

First Choice

Alternative One

Alternative Two

In the begynnynge of May a good flye. the body of roddyd wull and lappid
abowte wyth blacke sylke: the wynges of the drake & of the redde capons hakyll.

128

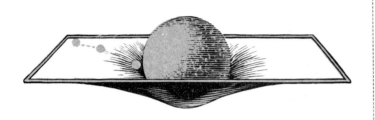

Writers on relativity theory often explain it in the following way. Imagine a rubber sheet stretched out flat like a trampoline. A grapefruit placed on this sheet will make a depression. A marble placed near the grapefruit will roll toward it. The grapefruit is not "pulling" the marble. Rather it has created a field (the depression) of such a structure that the marble, taking the path of least resistance, rolls toward the grapefruit. In a roughly (very roughly) similar way, space-time is curved or warped by the presence of large masses like the sun. This warping is the gravitational field. A planet moving around the sun is not moving in an ellipse because the sun pulls on it, but because the field is such that the ellipse is the straightest possible path the planet can take in space-time.

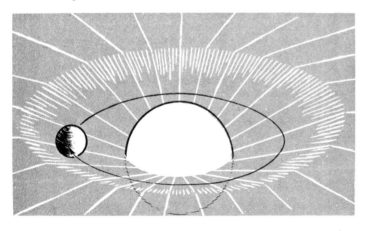

ANTHONY RAVIELLI
Relativity for the Million,
line in color separation,
6⅛ × 9¼ inches, 1962

Anthony Ravielli transforms scientific concepts into concrete and meaningful illustration in an apparently easy manner. He makes Martin Gardner's *Relativity for the Million* lucid and exciting with an abundance of drawings that reveal the artist's personal involvement in picturing scientific problems. He presents a human point of view—with people participating or with realistic objects and symbols designed in a lively fashion. His line style has the flowing tonal qualities found in his painting. The second color drawn on an overlay provides the highlights. Pictured here are contrasting explanations of the theory of relativity. The reader could set one up as an experiment at home. The other, more abstract, invites pondering.

Rarely does the reader find this human touch in technical illustration. It comes naturally to Ravielli—he has divided his interests between people and science. After having devoted many years to portrait painting and magazine illustration, during World War II he created instruction murals for the Second Service Command. Afterwards he applied this storytelling method of teaching to medical texts and to the writing and illustration of his own intriguing books, *Wonders of The Human Body* and *An Adventure in Geometry*.

The Higher Plants

ZONATION OF AQUATIC PLANTS

Water plants tend to grow in a definite pattern of zonation. This pattern is often quite regular.

1. Emergent water plants. These are rooted in the soil with their lower portions submersed. Some grow commonly in marshes or on the shore, though they may stand in as much as 6 to 7 feet of water. Most of their photosynthetic tissues are emergent. They are used for food and shelter by many water-loving animals, and as a means of entry and exit to and from the water.

2. Floating plants. These plants form a zone farther out in the water in depths ranging from a few inches to 8 or 9 feet. Most are rooted but a few are free-floating.

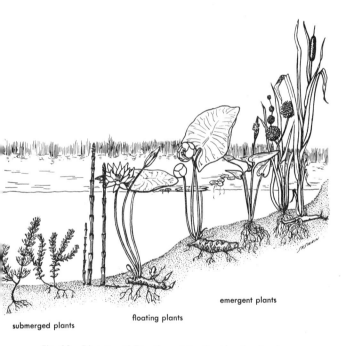

submerged plants

floating plants

emergent plants

Fig. 19. Diagram of Zonation at the Margin of a Pond.

SUZAN NOGUCHI SWAIN
The New Field Book of Freshwater Life,
line drawings and watercolor,
4⁹⁄₁₆ × 7¼ inches, 1966

One has only to look at Elsie B. Klot's *The New Field Book of Freshwater Life* to appreciate the artist's contribution. There are seven hundred drawings of aquatic plants, animals, and the equipment for collecting these specimens. When illustrations in scientific books are excellent, one recognizes the artist has a knowledge of and an enthusiasm for the subject equal to the author's. SuZan Noguchi Swain's interest in science began in college where she studied both illustration and biology. Her first book assignment was painting and drawing for Ralph W. Swain's *Insect Guide.* Subsequently she illustrated Alexander B. and Elsie B. Klot's *Living Insects of the World* and Edwin Way Teale's *Strange Ways of Familiar Insects.*

SuZan Noguchi Swain takes great pride in preparing her drawings "of nature's creatures from the living thing." For this miniature scene she draws the plants at the shore of a pond. Instantly one recognizes them and is made aware of the ecology.

At times she keeps specimens alive in her home, although this has presented problems. For this field book Elsie B. Klot gave her a gift of a stonefly nymph which she kept in a small aquarium, feeding it and watching its behavior. As the time drew near for the final drawing of the ventral view where the gills are found, the artist knew she would have to kill it. "Just about then the nymph became sluggish and as soon as it died, I drew it—relieved that it died rather than being killed by me for 'educational purpose.'"

She also works from specimens preserved in alcohol, dried insects, and occasionally, good photographs.

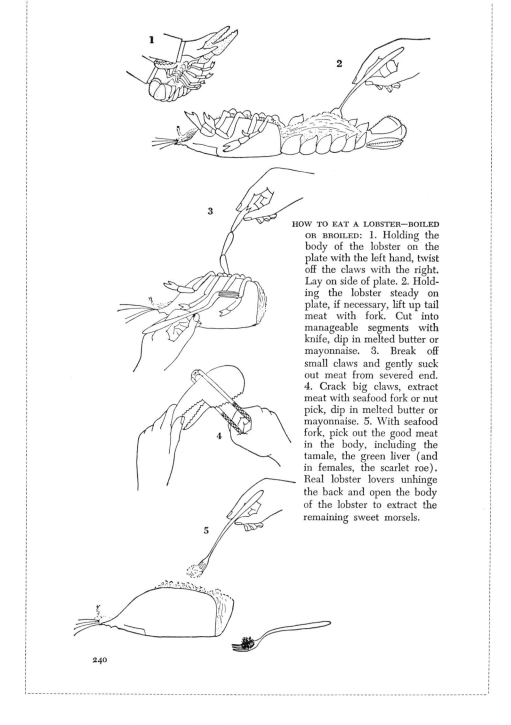

HOW TO EAT A LOBSTER—BOILED OR BROILED: 1. Holding the body of the lobster on the plate with the left hand, twist off the claws with the right. Lay on side of plate. 2. Holding the lobster steady on plate, if necessary, lift up tail meat with fork. Cut into manageable segments with knife, dip in melted butter or mayonnaise. 3. Break off small claws and gently suck out meat from severed end. 4. Crack big claws, extract meat with seafood fork or nut pick, dip in melted butter or mayonnaise. 5. With seafood fork, pick out the good meat in the body, including the tamale, the green liver (and in females, the scarlet roe). Real lobster lovers unhinge the back and open the body of the lobster to extract the remaining sweet morsels.

MARY SUZUKI   *Amy Vanderbilt's Complete Book of Etiquette,*
line drawings, 6⅛ × 9¼ inches, 1954

Illustrations for an etiquette book should be informative, explicit, and above all, in good taste. Mary Suzuki, whose interest is in fashion drawing and sewing illustration, possesses a sense of style that graces *Amy Vanderbilt's Complete Book of Etiquette.* Meticulously, in five simple steps, she makes the eating of a lobster enjoyable. She can draw a practical sequence of bedmaking or she can create a wedding ceremony, receiving line and bride's table in diagrams that impart a touch of elegance to the models.

EARL THOLLANDER
Delights and Prejudices,
wash drawings,
5⅜ × 9⅜ inches, 1964

When the California artist and painter Earl
Thollander accepts an assignment, he is likely
to visit the country or place concerned, if he
hasn't already been there, to sketch the sur-
rounding landscape, the people, their goods and
houses. For James Beard's culinary autobiography, Thollander takes us to the author's native
Oregon, to San Francisco, and St. Thomas as
well as to excellent restaurants.

He brings the mouth-watering ingredients
for preparing James Beard's recipes straight
from the markets. In strong line brushed with
wash to add "color" and texture Thollander
draws the sliced onion. We can almost smell its
aroma. In the same technique his other still
lifes show fresh broccoli, a shiny cucumber,
succulent blackberries, ripe peaches and pears,
and brook trout with a measuring cup brim-
ming with the makings of ginger sauce beside
it. When James Beard states, "I believe that
thickish cuts of meat are best for grilling . . .,"
Thollander produces the right cut of steak—
well-marbled with fat for flavor—the garlic,
and the essential carving knife and fork. In this
day of frozen and packaged food, it is refreshing to have this visual guide to first-rate
produce.

Earl Thollander is adept at showing the
techniques of preparation and the finished
dishes and does this expertly for Gloria Bley
Miller's *Thousand Recipe Chinese Cookbook*. His
book illustrations cover a large range of subjects and include the histories *South by South-
west* by John Tebbel and Ramon Ruiz and
Passage to the Golden Gate by Daniel Chu and
Samuel Chu. His jacket paintings, luscious in
color, could well be used as frontispieces.

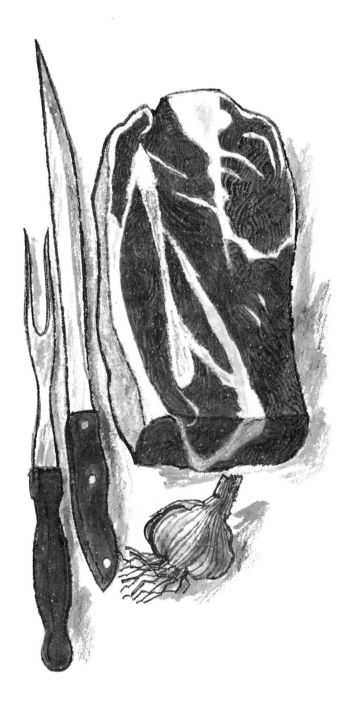

THE ART AND CRAFT OF ILLUSTRATION

Illustrating a book is a special and personal undertaking, which, when finished, gives you a sense of accomplishment and pleasure. Within the limitations of the book's size and shape, you, the artist, can express yourself in drawing or painting with much the same freedom as at your easel. Your illustration will be reproduced on another surface, will face the patterns of a page of type, and when bound in a cloth or paper case, will be a book that many readers will view without ever seeing your original drawings or paintings. Other graphic mediums, more flamboyant but ephemeral—the poster, the billboard, the record cover, the book jacket, the package design—always require the selling of an idea, a message, a product. Perhaps stage design comes closest to book illustration. That is why Eugene Berman, Domenico Gnoli, and John Piper, who designed for the stage, subsequently turned to book illustration. Stage settings have to be functional with areas for furniture and for actors to perform in whereas book illustrations remain unchanged as the artist envisioned and created them.

The greatest experience for the artist is illustrating and fabricating a book. It may be just the one copy but it will be recognized as a book. For adult illustration or for children's books, the first step is choosing a story or poem that appeals to you and then deciding upon the book size. Draw or paint your illustrations and handwrite or indicate the text area on separate sheets which can be assembled in a portfolio. Or you might tape the pages at the back to form an accordian-pleated dummy. Or even sew them together and then glue them along the back to a handmade binding.

Ben Shahn, before submitting a book idea to a publisher, always made a sample book to get the feel of its proportions and to visualize the pace of his storytelling. In his studio I first saw, as a small crudely bound dummy, his last book, *For the Sake of a Single Verse*, recently published as a large art portfolio. As I looked inside the dummy, the art and the handwritten text were of such perfection that they could have been sent to the printer as final copy ready for the camera, the first step in reproduction. On all of his books, Shahn worked with the same dedication and interest that he had on the design of his first book, an experience he emotionally described in his *Love and Joy about Letters*. "Sometime during the thirties I designed my first book, and I undertook the project as a chore. But then I began to discover the delights of type: fitness, elegance, tradition, humor, the color of pages, the vast panorama of choices, each with its own peculiar flavor which added so much to the words said. I enjoyed a year or so of complete infatuation with type. . . . If my enthusiasm cooled, that was because I began to realize that the uses and the understanding of type are a life's work, and that I would never be much more than a dabbler."

In the nineteen-fifties, Leonard Baskin sometimes took folded signatures, the unbound pages that make up a book, and, in them, sketched his ideas before preparing his final art. He considered the paperback cover an important part of the book and planned it with dignity. Figure 1 shows Baskin's sketch for *The Last Days of Shelley & Byron* and figure 2 the final printed cover.

Before accepting a book assignment Warren Chappell reads the manuscript. When he submits sketches, he also outlines the entire *mise en pages*—the front and back matter, the text pages, the endpaper design, the binding, even the

Figure 1   Cover sketch, line drawing

Figure 2   Printed cover, line in color separation

Figure 3   Title page sketch, line drawing

Figure 4   Final art, line drawing

jacket. They are freely drawn to indicate the direction the final art will take. If sketches are too finished, the completed art looks tight and contrived. I quote from Warren Chappell's letter to me about *The Fairy Ring*: "I'm sure you realize that I can't do sketches which I feel are more than indications of style and subject. The jacket should *always* come last, and it seems a shame, always to disregard so obvious an imperative. . . . The ornament which will be made up for jacket and binding spines is by no means clearly formed in my mind—I think that the right sort of floret can also be used as a spot in connection with special opening pages for each of the selections." In Figures 3 and 4 note the rendering for the title page and the exquisite final drawing to which type was added. For the text page in Figure 5 Chappell indicates the type area in relation to the illustration.

I have just given a glimpse of how the professional artist works at making a book. Now let me explain the necessary details about the preparation of art for book publication and the mediums you, the artist, might work in to adapt your art to the book. I will tell briefly about the printing processes in order to help you understand why you must follow certain procedures in drawing and painting.

I cannot stress enough that the prerequisite for illustration is an ability to draw. You should be so at ease with pen or brush that the restrictions of medium, size, and area imposed by the book do not hamper your style. Everything you have seen, known, read, or studied will be of value. Start by keeping a sketch-book handy and carrying a pen at all times. Continually add observations of the

Figure 5   Sketches for text and illustration, line drawing

THE WHITE CAT   105

world around you—people walking or sitting, animals at home or in the zoo, street scenes, buildings, interiors with people and furniture, cityscapes, landscapes, seascapes. These fragments capturing a mood or moment will be potential storytelling scenes. Finished drawings in ink can be prepared from these sketches in your studio and collected in a portfolio for future showing. Even assign yourself a novel, a travel book, or a cookbook to illustrate. Remember Lynd Ward wrote novels in woodcuts.

Although watercolor is rarely used for adult illustration, you might be asked to prepare the jacket in color. Try to find time to paint because it adds new viewpoints to your line style and it strengthens your handling of a wash drawing in black alone. Leonard Rosoman commented on this need to me, "I think I regard myself as a painter who is interested in illustration—I would almost go to the length of saying that it is necessary for an illustrator to be a painter." Edward Ardizzone, also a watercolorist, is represented in museum collections, and has illustrated many books in color.

Line Drawings

Most likely your first assignment will be a number of line drawings to be done in very black ink such as Higgins Super Black or Artone Extra Dense and on paper or board that is pure, clean white, not ivory or cream. In my selection of illustrations note the variety of line styles—the detailed line of Bernarda Bryson and the flowing line of Eugene Karlin. For the publisher the line drawing is most economical because, when made into a line cut, it can print with the text on a paper suitable for letterpress printing. If you think of letterpress printing as type pressing on the paper, you will always remember that your drawings must be as clean-cut and sharp as the metal type, thus in a line style. Your finished drawings are sent to the engraver where they are photographed and the negative film is exposed on a zinc or copper plate and etched. That is, the non-printing areas are chemically removed, leaving the printing areas in positive form. These plates are then locked together with the text page to make printing plates for the entire book.

Before starting an assignment, examine other books produced by the publisher. Inquire about the kind of paper your drawing will be printed on and draw accordingly for its texture and color. Will the line drawings print from metal, plastic, or rubber plates? Rubber plate printing has shortcomings. As the plates press on the paper, the lines thicken and many fine lines in a small area tend to

Figure 6   Illustration sketch, line drawing

run together. Large areas of black do not print as a solid black but as a mottled mass. Even with these limitations you can make a handsome book. Topolski adapted to it and to groundwood paper for *Pygmalion*. Betty Fraser prepared her illustrations for Marjorie Holmes's *I've Got to Talk to Somebody, God* for rubber plate printing. In Figure 6 her pencil sketch for the second chapter is a mere indication of subject matter and is drawn to book size to fit within the text area. Her final drawing in Figure 7 is same or actual size. If she had worked one third

Figure 7   Final art, line drawing for rubber plate printing

larger or twice size, her fine lines might have filled up and become patchy black areas in reduction. She drew in Pelican Black ink on white two-ply bristol paper. Beneath the drawing she has added a blocking line so that the engraver would know at what angle to block the line cut and the printer would position it accordingly with the text type. Otherwise a drawing could be printed upside down in error.

The size you choose to draw your final art depends on how you like to work. It causes the publisher considerable inconvenience in handling and additional expense in reproduction if you work three or four times as large as the final book. If working same size seems too confining, try twice size or one third larger for greater freedom. Whatever the size, all drawings must be made in the same focus. Establish a working area by drawing its outline on tracing paper. If you redraw, check the area with the tracing paper outline so that your drawings don't get larger and larger. If you work in dry brush or scratchboard for line reproduction, work actual size so that the character of your drawing will be retained in reproduction. Scratchboard involves painting a chalk-coated bristol board in black and scratching away the areas you wish to be in white.

The drawings may extend beyond the text area but rarely bleed to the edge of the page. If the composition is a doublespread continuing across facing pages, it is best not to make the center the focal point. Sometimes important details are lost to the eye in the center, or gutters, because the bound book does not open perfectly flat. Often another quarter of an inch is lost in the center in library rebinding.

Choose a paper or board to work on that is substantial enough to take corrections and handling. Try not to draw to the very edge of the paper so that there is room for the art director and the book designer to mark sizes and write instructions to the engraver. When you wish to correct a line drawing, paint over it in china white. Or do the correction on another surface and paste it in position on the original. When Betty Fraser makes a correction, she rubs out with an ink or electric eraser the line she wishes to change and draws over the bare area.

Woodcuts, Linoleum Cuts, Wood Engravings

The more you experiment in drawing mediums similar to letterpress printing, the more experienced you will become in creating a perfect line drawing. Work with woodcuts, linoleum blocks, or wood engravings and prove them by hand in your studio. You will realize that every line made will be printed, that the line has to be even in weight to print well, and that nothing can be added or corrected once the block has been cut. So in commercial engraving, once the line cut has been made, there can be no changes. For a woodcut draw on a soft wood and cut away the area you do not wish printed. The linoleum block is made the same way. For a wood engraving, sketch on an end-grain slab of boxwood and with a burin cut away the areas that are not to print. With all three mediums the image is in relief like a piece of metal or wooden type. If you illustrate with wood or linoleum cuts or wood engravings you will need to provide the publisher with hand-pulled proofs for line reproduction. It is not practical to print from the original woodcut or linoleum block except in very small quantities. The woodcut or linoleum block soon wears out.

The woodcut offers you a chance to experiment with rudimentary color separation. You will learn that transparent inks mix in printing in much the same way as your watercolors do in painting. For a two-color print in black and red, make a woodcut for each color. Prove the red first, then, in register, prove the black. Where the black overprints the red, a richer black is achieved. If you wish a red pattern to drop out of the black, cut away those areas on the woodcut from the black plate. Use that second color sparingly. *The Second Color* by Richard S. Coyne and Robert M. Blanchard will show you how black and a second color combine. Their book *The Third Color* will show how two colors other than black print.

Beware! Do not become so immersed in the craft of printmaking that you forget to communicate—to tell the story in pictures with feeling. The artist, not the technique, should be the master. Antonio Frasconi, Seong Moy, and Joseph Low, who have explored the medium of the print, skillfully prepare their art in this way for the book publisher.

It would be helpful if all artists could visit an engraver or a printer. These busy professionals often do not have time to show artists around nor are their plants always accessible. However, do visit the local newspaper plant and the small job printer who handles signs, letterheads, and brochures. And do make an effort to read Marshall Lee's *Bookmaking*, Hugh Williamson's *Methods of Book Design*, and Victor Strauss's *The Printing Industry*.

Two-Color Line Drawings

Equally brilliant results in two-color line are achieved by mastery of pen or dry brush. For the cover of *The Old Curiosity Shop* Robin Jacques painted a sketch in two colors, keeping in mind color separation for his final art. In Figures 8, 9, and 10 examine the preparation of the final art in two steps and the printed cover; Jacques drew the black plate same size on bristol paper and added register marks. For the second color he drew and painted in black on a translucent overlay of Dietzgen drafting film, a material that could be seen through and that would not curl or shrink with temperature changes or with the application of ink or paint. By adding register marks to both the black plate and the overlay before you draw, you will always know where the colors appear. While working on the overlay, you are free to turn and add a detail to the black plate and then return to the overlay without checking positions in a light box. These register marks also serve as a guide in platemaking. Today a newer method, the pin-register system, eliminates the need of a light box and register marks. The art director provides translucent overlay sheets punched at the top with holes to hold small pins. You tape the pins to your drawing board and slip the overlays over them. As you work from one overlay to another, your art is always in register.

    If you cannot work in line and draw only in wash or pencil, tell the art director. Perhaps the budget will allow halftone drawings on coated stock or the

Figure 9   Final art, line drawing for second color

Figure 8   Final art, line drawing for black plate

book will be printed by offset, a more economical process for halftone reproduction. If the specifications for line drawings cannot be changed, it is better not to accept the assignment. You might damage an author's book as well as your own reputation.

Wash Drawings, Pencil Drawings

Halftone art as distinct from line art can be printed by letterpress if the publisher provides at additional cost a coated or smooth finish paper. Halftone means that the drawing strokes in black made with pencil, brush, or pen vary in tone from solid black to the palest grey. The engraver must photograph the drawing through a halftone screen, with a grid of fine lines, transforming the art into a mass of tiny dots. The size of the clear dot on the negative varies from ten percent in the highlights of your drawing to fifty percent in the middle tones and to ninety percent in the shadow or darker areas. When the negative film is printed on a copper or zinc engraving, to make the halftone cut a reversal takes place. The highlights print a pinpoint dot of black, the middle tones a fifty percent dot of black, and the shadow or darker tones approach ninety percent to solid black. The halftone cut is then locked together with the type for printing.

Figure 10   Printed illustration, line in color separation

When you make a wash drawing use either water-soluble black ink, such as Pelican "Fount" or a waterproof black ink such as Pelican Black, Artone extra dense, or Higgins Super Black, or paint with Winsor Newton Lamp black or jet black. They all produce excellent results on bristol illustration board or water-color paper. If you use a second color, always add register marks to the key plate and translucent overlay. If you combine wash with line, paint the wash on the key plate and draw the black line on an overlay. In this way the drawing will be photographed as a combination line and halftone and the line will be sharp, not broken up into little dots. A pencil drawing calls for a very black pencil. You might try Eagle prismacolor, Eagle verithin, or Eagle thinex, but stay away from charcoal, pencil, lithographic crayon or graphite pencil. However, Robert Osborn has always worked with lithographic crayon and can handle it properly for reproduction. Study his *Mankind May Never Make It!*

Take care when making corrections on original halftone art as every pencil line, redrawing, or fingerprint will be caught by the camera. Do not paint out an area for correction in white. Instead carefully scrape the surface clear with a razor blade or remove with a mild bleach solution of one part bleach to four parts water. For corrections on an overlay use a glass eraser. Always work on a large enough surface. If additional areas of sky or water are needed you have room to add them. If you try to join extra board to your original the camera will pick up the line formed by the joining of the two surfaces.

Offset lithography allows greater freedom in materials and drawing area without additional expense in platemaking for the book publisher. You may paint in black wash, draw in pencil, or combine line and wash in one composition. If you request a silhouette halftone, the platemaker "whites out" the half-tone background area you have indicated to be removed on a tissue overlay over your art. Your drawing then prints against a clear background. In Figure 11 Earl Thollander made a combination wash and line drawing. The art appears silhouetted in Gloria Bley Miller's *The Thousand Recipe Chinese Cookbook*. Your drawing may "bleed" or extend to the very edge of the book page as in Osborn's watercolors for *Osborn on Leisure*. For "bleed" art provide another quarter inch of painting on all four sides beyond the trim size of the book. The binder then has leeway in trimming the printed sheets. Be sure to ask if your art can bleed. The printer has to order a larger sheet of printing paper so that the gripper edge of the printing press will not touch inside the art area.

With offset lithography you may take full responsibility for the *mise en pages*, the arrangement of type and illustration. After the offset platemaker photographs the type and the art, he joins or "strips" the negative film as one

Figure 11 Final art, line and wash drawing

unit to be transferred to the printing plate rather than locking together metal
type with the halftone cut for letterpress printing. Offset lithography stems from
the lithographic process developed in the early nineteenth century. The offset
plate is so prepared that the printing areas accept ink and the non-printing areas
repel ink. The plate does not print directly on the paper but on a rubber blanket
which "offsets" the image of type and art on coated or non-coated paper.
The making of a lithograph in your studio will help you understand the princi-

ples of offset lithography and also the technique of color separation. Draw with a grease crayon on a specially prepared limestone, zinc, or paper plate, the printing plate. Dampen the surface with water so that the non-printing areas repel ink. Roll a greasy ink over this surface and prove your drawing with its tone and textures on a piece of paper.

Drawing for Direct Contact

If your pencil or dry brush drawings are made same size on a translucent or thin material, the art will not be photographed but will be transferred by direct contact to the printing plate. After sketches have been approved, make a sample final drawing. The production department might make a trial plate and show proofs.

Your drawing paper should be thin, very white and with a grainlike two-ply bristol paper or the translucent Dietzgen drafting film or Technifax hydropel TVP. Their surface texture breaks up the pencil lines into a range of tones similar to drawing on a lithographic stone. Draw the key plate in black on the two-ply bristol and, if there is a second color, draw it in black in register on the translucent overlay. On the overlay provide a one-inch-square swatch of the second color from an International Printing Inks or P.M.S. (Pantone Matching System) sample book. Choose a coated sample for coated book paper or a non-coated sample for non-coated paper. If you cannot find the second color you wish, paint a two-inch square of the solid color for matching. Do not overpaint in white prior to making a correction. On the bristol paper use a razor blade ever so lightly for minor corrections; deep scratches will reproduce as a line. On the translucent material wash off the ink; if Technifax hydropel TVP, erase the pencil lines.

The platemaker then passes a strong light through the drawings. The image is exposed directly to the photographic film from which a plate is made. This method retains the texture and detail of your original drawings.

Full Color

All artists would like to paint in full color, that is using a complete palette of watercolors including black on a white surface. Whether the printing process is letterpress or offset, the first step in reproducing full color art is photography. Art directors permit full color painting when the book budget can afford the cost of four-color platemaking. Today a large percentage of full color art is separated electronically. The platemaker photographs the red in your painting with a green filter, the yellow with a blue filter, and the blue with a red filter. He separates the black from your painting by using filters for a portion of the exposure time. The individual negatives are used to produce the four plates which print in the process colors of yellow, magenta, cyan blue, and black to create, not an exact reproduction but a splendid resemblance of your original art.

If you work in full color prepare a sample painting for the art director to check size and quality of color. Paint on a white, two-ply bristol illustration board or watercolor paper with transparent and opaque watercolors or tempera. If your composition has fine black lines, draw these on an overlay in register with the key painting. In this way your lines will be reproduced sharply as line, not broken up into dots by the halftone screen. The other colors will be clear and bright because there is no black halftone to muddy them. Do not add highlights in oil, Dr. Martin's dyes, a felt pen, or gold paint. As you work in one medium, the camera catches the full range of color. If you mix mediums, it is difficult for the camera to separate the texture and brilliance of Dr. Martin's dyes or the felt pens from the watercolor. The process inks do not duplicate the vivid magentas, pinks, and purples or the vibrant, sparkling greens and blues. Use china white only for corrections. If you work entirely in oil, the art will be accepted. Remember the time-consuming drying and try to avoid the problems created by large size canvases in reduction.

Art in Color Separation

Don't be afraid of pre-separating your own art rather than painting in full color. This is usually done by making a drawing or painting for each of four colors including black in register on successive overlays. It is time consuming but if you learn color separation, you will have the chance to create full-color book illustration with individual and beautiful color of your own choosing rather than with process colors. In time, hopefully, book publishers will use more color for all books. As Paul Hogarth says in *Creative Ink Drawing*, "This is not as mechanical a procedure as it may sound. I find that I am still discovering better ways of making a texture or a more interesting shape in my separations, right up to the time I should be mailing my finished art to the client." The reason for the preparation of art in four-color separation is that the removal of black from a painting by camera and the subsequent photographing with three other colored filters is an expensive procedure. Your color separations reduce the cost of color plates and make book illustrations in color economically possible. Edward Bawden, a master at color separation, used with wizardry the English material plastocowell for his *Gulliver's Travels*. Lynton Lamb prepared his "paintings" for *Tono-Bungay* in four-color separation. Again, making a lithograph, woodcut, or engraving in several colors in your studio will help you understand color separation. Draw on a different stone or transfer paper for each of the four colors with a grease crayon and prove the drawings on stone or transfer paper in register to make your color print.

The First Method

There are three different methods of four-color separation. They require all the steps I have described previously, and you will already have mastered the preparation of line or halftone art. Start by painting a sketch in full color. The first method gives you complete control of the texture and range of colors. Follow the principles of two-color separation shown in Figures 8 and 9, that is, drawing in line or wash the black plate and on three successive overlays in solid black the line or flat color areas for the other three colors. Label your colors and attach color swatches for matching. For a paler tone of one color, prepare it in solid black on a fifth overlay and label it fifty percent of the color. If you would like to use wash or pencil on one or more of the overlays, seek the advice of the art director. The use of halftone increases the plate cost. As you draw in pencil, you will learn which pencil makes a solid black tone and which will create seventy-five, fifty, or twenty-five percent of black for use on halftone overlays. As you prepare each overlay, refer to your sketch so that you do not omit an essential color area on a particular overlay. If you are not sure how colors mix and overprint, borrow from the art director a process color-printing chart which shows how these colors combine in varying percentages. To create brown the printer uses one hundred percent yellow, fifty percent magenta, fifty percent cyan blue, and ten percent black. To create a bright, light green he uses one hundred percent yellow and sixty percent cyan blue. As you work on your overlays, equate your color palette to the values of the process colors. If the printer makes a sample color proof, you can create your own chart. On your key plate and on each overlay paint a border in tones of black ranging from one hundred percent to ten percent. Arrange the borders so that they overlap. In proof you can study how your pen or brush creates the colors in varying strengths and hues. It is helpful to purchase a strong loupe. With it you can examine pre-separated or process colors in reproduction. You will learn how percentages of color combine to make the colors you have painted.

The Second Method

Choose the second method if you are more at ease in painting. Make your key painting in color or the three process colors and add the black on a transparent overlay. By mixing the three process colors—magenta, cyan blue and process yellow—you can create any color needed, even black. On a translucent overlay with register marks you add the black line needed for highlights and emphasis. If you wish areas of black tone, on another overlay paint in black wash. If you combine the black line with the black wash on one overlay, the line photographed through the grid for halftone will not be solid. When your art is printed, the printer will use only the three process colors plus black to reproduce your entire palette of colors.

The Third Method

The third method of color separation is best if you like to compose in black and apply color afterwards. You prepare in drawing or painting your black plate with register marks. The platemaker proves it in non-photographic blue on three-ply bristol and provides a black proof on acetate. On the non-photographic blue proof you paint with a palette of three primary colors. As you work, flip the black acetate over the painting so that you can visualize the final results. Figure 12 shows how Robin Jacques drew in black line. On the non-photographic blue, Figure 13, he painted in watercolor without black. The printed effect is a full color painting for Charles Edward Carryl's "A Capital Ship."

Figure 12   Final art, line drawing for black plate

Figure 13   Final art, watercolor without black line

And we all felt ill as mariners will,
    On a diet that's cheap and rude;
And we shivered and shook as we dipped the cook
    In a tub of his gluesome food.
Then nautical pride we laid aside,
    And we cast the vessel ashore
On the Gulliby Isles, where the Poohpooh smiles,
    And the Anagazanders roar.

82

Figure 14 Printed illustration, watercolor in separation

Mise en pages

Become aware now of the *mise en pages* of the entire book. Its history can be traced as far back as the illuminated manuscript. Only then will you appreciate your contribution in illustration to the overall plan of the book.

Usually there is a binding design which you may or may not be asked to do. Warren Chappell is partial to decorating the spine or backbone and its front cover. Inside the book the endsheet may be in flat color or decorated with scenes, charts, or a map. The front matter which introduces an author's work usually includes in the following order:

half title	*table of contents*
card plate	*list of illustrations*
title page	*foreword*
copyright page	*preface*
dedication (or epigraph)	*introduction*
acknowledgments	*second half title or first part title*

You might contribute a frontispiece to face the title page as the late Miguel Covarrubias did for *Mexico South* or a doublespread extending across both pages and allowing room for the title, author's name and publisher's imprint on the right-hand page. Small decorations may be placed at the head of the contents, introduction, and second half title. Erik Blegvad painted a part title scene in watercolor around "Country Life" for *The* Margaret Rudkin *Pepperidge Farm Cookbook.*

Within the text there are many variations in size and layout for the illustration. Rockwell Kent does compact storytelling scenes at the opening of each chapter in *N by E,* whereas Victor Ambrus handles one simple element in *A Glimpse of Eden.* Lynd Ward fits half-page drawings within the text of *Gargantua & Pantagruel.* Philip Reisman prefers single or full-page drawings for the small format of *Crime and Punishment.* Susanne Suba allows space for captions in *Morning Faces* as does John Langley Howard in *The Origins of Angling.* Henry C. Pitz paints a double spread that bleeds for Froissart's *Chronicles.*

The back matter with it's appendixes, glossary, bibliography, index, and colophon, occasionally has decorative headings for the glossary and index. A decoration at the end of a chapter or on the last page of a book is a tailpiece.

Assignments

Book assignments vary with the publisher's instructions to provide twenty pages of illustrations placed throughout the manuscript as you wish or specific requests for a frontispece, eight part titles, an illustration for each chapter, and several "spot" drawings. You will be given a copy of the manuscript to read and to work with. Jot down the page number of the manuscript on both your sketch and final drawing. The author might provide research material that can prove invaluable. If not, you are responsible for it. You will need to do considerable research for some books. Anthony Gross spent six months in study before starting his drawings for *The Forsyte Saga*. The New York Public Library has a picture collection just for artists. Magazines provide tear sheets of articles. Newspaper offices have extensive photographic files. *Picture Sources*, edited by Celestine G. Frankenburg, lists references for picture research. In your own home keep a file of pictures and collect reference books.

Do not begrudge sketches—they can be a mere suggestion of what you are going to draw. If they are to be looked at by the author of the book you are illustrating, ask your questions and add any explanations in the margins. The editor and author can point out incorrect details in dress or architecture which in the final art could be difficult to change. At times there will be too much interference; you, the artist, have the privilege of saying "No" to too many changes.

If your illustrations are for a picture book, do rough sketches so that the designer can set the text to complement your *mise en pages*. When you receive the type proofs make a dummy of text and illustration. Antonio Frasconi planned a complete dummy for *Bestiary/Bestiario* as did Joseph Low for *Directions to Servants*. A dummy helps you check the order of front matter, text, and back matter, the size of art, and, if the pages alternate two-color with four-color illustration, the color imposition provided by the bookbinder.

I have outlined the many steps in illustrating a book and have commented on some of the problems that might arise. I have based these directions on my experience in working with many artists. Each book you illustrate will teach you more about the mediums to work in and the printing processes. Work out your style at your own pace. The completed book should be a joy to you and to every reader. Each illustrated book is as much a work of art as a painting or drawing.

BIBLIOGRAPHY

Books

Aesop FIVE CENTURIES OF ILLUSTRATED FABLES. Selected by John J. McKendry. New York, 1964.

The Artist and the Book, 1860–1960 in Western Europe and the United States. Boston, 1961.

BLAND, DAVID. *A History of Book Illustration.* Cleveland, 1958.

CHAPPELL, WARREN. *Sixty-Three Drawings*, with a comment by Isabel Bishop and a checklist by Eleanor Steiner-Prag. New York, 1955.

W.A.D. (Dwiggins, W. A.). *MSS.* New York, 1947.

From Sickert to 1948. With a commentary by John Russell. London, 1948.

GILL, BOB, and LEWIS, JOHN. *Illustrations: Aspects and Directions.* New York, 1964.

HOGARTH, PAUL. *The Artist as Reporter.* New York, 1967.

———— *Creative Ink Drawing.* New York, 1968.

Homage to the Book. Foreword by Frederick B. Adams, Jr. New York, 1968.

Images of Dignity: The Drawings of Charles White. Foreword by Harry Belafonte, introduction by James Porter, commentary by Benjamin Horowitz. Los Angeles, 1967.

JOHNSON, UNA E., and MILLER, JO. *American Graphic Artists of the Twentieth Century.* Monograph No. 2 (Isabel Bishop). New York, 1964.

LAMB, LYNTON. *Drawing for Illustration.* London, 1962.

LEE, MARSHALL. *Bookmaking: The Illustrated Guide to Design & Production.* New York, 1965.

LEWIS, JOHN. *A Handbook of Type and Illustration.* London, 1956.

———— *The Twentieth Century Book.* New York, 1967.

MCLEAN, RUARI. *Modern Book Design.* Fair Lawn, New Jersey, 1959.

MELCHER, DANIEL, and LARRICK, NANCY. *Printing and Promotion Handbook.* New York, 1956.

PITZ, HENRY C. *The Brandywine Tradition.* Boston, 1969.

Portrait of Latin America as Seen by Her Print Makers. Edited by Anne Lyon Haight, with foreword by Monroe Wheeler and introduction by Jean Charlot. New York, 1946.

Quarto-Millenary. New York, 1959.

RENARD, JULES. *Natural History.* Cambridge, 1960.

SACHS, PAUL J. *Modern Prints and Drawings.* New York, 1954.

SHAHN, BEN. *Love and Joy about Letters.* New York, 1963.

STRAUSS, VICTOR. *The Printing Industry.* Washington, D.C., 1967.

WHEELER, MONROE. *Modern Painters and Sculptors as Illustrators*. New York, 1946.
WILLIAMSON, HUGH. *Methods of Book Design*. London, 1956.

Articles

BARMAN, CHRISTIAN, "The Return of Illustration," in R. B. Fishenden, ed.,
    The Penrose Annual, XLVII (New York, 1953), 15–19.
EICHENBERG, FRITZ, "Robert Osborn, Cartoonist with Teeth," in *American Institute of
    Graphic Arts Journal*, III, 4 (1951), 21–23.
FLOWER, DESMOND, "The Book Illustrations of E. McKnight Kauffer," in
    R. B. Fishenden, ed., *The Penrose Annual*, L (New York, 1956), 35–40.
GREEN, TIMOTHY, "Topolski's Coronation," in *Horizon*, III, 2 (November 1960),
    128–136.
KING, DOROTHY, "Notes on the Gehenna Press," in *Printing & Graphic Arts*, VII, 2
    (June 1959), 33–48.
LOW, JOSEPH, "Notes on the Eden Hill Press," in *Printing & Graphic Arts*, VIII, 2
    (June 1960), 21–30.
PIPER, JOHN, "Book Illustration and the Painter-Artist," in R. B. Fishenden, ed.,
    The Penrose Annual, XLIII (London, 1949), 52–54.
ROSNER, CHARLES, "Art Is Indivisible," in R. B. Fishenden, ed., *The Penrose Annual*,
    L (New York, 1956), 41–44.
Speaking of Pictures . . . "Ex-Navy Artist Lampoons Art of War," in *Life*,
    January 27, 1947, pages 14–16.
WECKSLER, SALLY, "Books in the Making," in *Publisher's Weekly*, December 5, 1960,
    pages 64–65

INDEX